WHAT ISN'T THERE

WHAT ISN'T THERE

INSIDE A SEASON OF CHANGE

A JOURNAL

JOCELYN LIEU

Nation Books
New York

WHAT ISN'T THERE
Inside a Season of Change

Copyright © 2007 by Jocelyn Lieu

Published by
Nation Books
A Member of the Perseus Books Group

Nation Books is a copublishing venture of the Nation Institute and
Avalon Publishing Group, Incorporated.

Library of Congress Cataloging-in-Publication Data is available.

ISBN-13: 978-1-56858-346-4

9 8 7 6 5 4 3 2 1

Book design by Maria Fernandez
Printed in the United States of America

*We are grateful for the words that find us in our season
of not knowing.*
—GORDON DRAGT

*I want to sing. I want a language that I can lean on
and that can lean on me, that asks me to bear witness
and that I can ask to bear witness, to what power there
is in us to overcome this cosmic isolation.*
—MAHMOUD DARWISH

CONTENTS

PREFACE

When I began this book on September 11, 2001, I had no idea what I was doing. I barely remember writing the first sentences. Notions of craft and completion were the last things on my mind. They had become, in the space of one morning, impossible to imagine. All I knew, later that night, as my husband and I sat watching the news a mile and a half from the burning wreckage of the World Trade Center, was that I had to trap the bare truth of what I saw in words.

What I saw was beyond me. Time had slowed, crystallized. I can recall the exact appearance of the word "Live" suspended in the upper corner of the TV screen, but I have no memory of watching the first tower fall. Only in replay, repeated replay, could I begin to understand what I had seen. Only when it had stopped being live could the image sink in.

If to witness means to know by seeing, I was a lousy witness. Like most of us, I couldn't believe my eyes. This was New York City. For all of its relative dangers, it was, and still is, at least in my gentrifying neighborhood, a fairly tame place to live. Destruction on an epic scale just didn't happen here. While I realize now that it did and can—while I feel obliteration's nearness in ways I couldn't back then—I was, as we all were, stunned. And being stunned thrust me into a kind of holy timelessness where narrative continuity didn't exist. Each moment was isolated; each moment became a cell glowing with its own weird radiance. There was no way to string moments together, to make sense of things. Whenever I tried, my attempts seemed to violate the truth of the smoldering world outside.

By necessity, then, this book was written as a journal. Four years and several rounds of revision after its first drafting, it remains a kind of journal. While rewriting and shaping the moments captured in my notebooks, I found myself using some of the same tricks I'd learned as a fiction writer to tease out and give coherence to the flashes burned in memory, a process not unlike printing photographs taken in the blur of a catastrophe. I gave individual titles to the passages that emerged, and in some cases disguised the identities of my students, friends, and acquaintances by changing their names or attributes. That's about it for invention, though. Anything more obviously artful wouldn't convey what it was like to live through that time. It wouldn't be, in the deepest sense, true.

A journal is by nature fragmentary; *What Isn't There* thus is as much about absence as about what survives. Absence begins with the physical. The space in the sky where the towers once stood is filled with their non-presence. Painful awareness of the void is one reason why the Tribute of Light, the two powerful beams cast into the sky from the buildings' foundations, seems so right to many New Yorkers. It traces the contours of what used to exist, helping us to see what's gone.

*   *   *

Few may remember that when the term "Ground Zero" was first applied to the destroyed World Trade Center, it didn't stand for the ruins alone but encompassed all of Lower Manhattan.

Hearing the phrase increased my sense of doom. Figuratively speaking, we had been erased. "Ground Zero" was and still is the term used to define the site of impact of nuclear or other cataclysmic weapons, "weapons of mass destruction." Renamed, our neighborhood had stopped being a place and become an anti-place. We were reduced by language to ash and air. We had become the act of being bombed.

Within a week, the police cordons at Fourteenth Street lifted. The label "Ground Zero" shrank to enfold the disaster area itself. We were no longer cut off, literally or metaphorically, from the rest of the city, no longer quite one with destruction and death. We had left the zone of imagined erasure for no other reason than that we'd been renamed.

War is as much about language as it is about the deployment of weapons and movement of troops. If, as has been said, the militants who attacked the World Trade Center and Pentagon are to be judged on rhetoric alone, they scored a brilliant victory against U.S. economic and military domination. The White House joined the rhetorical battle, doing its best to seize 9/11 as a reason for waging worldwide war. That seizure has been challenged by peace groups, many of them, notably, based in New York.

It's not my intent to enter the war over symbols. I mention it because I hope to wage another.

In the days following September 11, almost everyone we saw—friends, neighbors, colleagues—told us where they'd been and what they'd been doing when the towers fell. Listening to them enabled me to blindly feel the contours of what's called the big picture. Listening also let me begin the work of understanding the then-private pictures darkening and taking shape inside of me.

By telling my story, the fractured story of a woman who lived on the ground once called Ground Zero, I hope, in a small way, to help rescue the day from symbolism. May it be returned to the realm of lived experience, which is where, if there is to be peace—the "fierce continual flame" of peace that the poet Muriel Rukeyser writes of—it belongs.

November 2006
New York City

I

IN THE LIFE AFTER

THE FIRST SIX DAYS

We have gathered here, on Second Avenue between Second and Third streets, because it's here the tenements part to offer the first real view of the World Trade Center.

Below the rising smoke, metal strands peel back like shredded skin. The air is so clear we can see the gleaming tines that surround each arched window. Much of the glass in the upper stories has been blown away. With the burning darkness inside, the towers look like blackened honeycombs.

In the stroller I hold tightly by the handles sits my eighteen-month-old daughter, Gracie. My husband, Chuck, stands behind us. Like several others in the crowd, I'm crying. Chuck makes no attempt to comfort me, nor do I want him to. What we see above us is larger than personal grief, larger than any attempt to assuage it.

A couple of people aim binoculars. Others have the silver or black disks of earphones inserted in their ears. And it seems that we should be able to hear the burning, but the blue sky is silent. The only sounds are the sirens, the police cars, fire trucks, and ambulances wailing down the avenue. Later I'll wonder how many of the rescue workers riding in those police cars, fire trucks, and ambulances died in the towers' collapse. I will try to visualize those vanished men, but all I'll really remember—if I'm not just imagining this—are a few blurred faces without identifying features. An impression, lost.

A car-service limo has pulled up to the curb. From its open window booms a radio newsman's voice. Straining to listen, I push the stroller closer.

The driver glances up at me. A white shirt open at the neck reveals a patch of smooth brown skin. Looking away, he turns up the volume.

The sound is now, for our sake, very loud, but because of the distortions it's hard to make out whole sentences. The Pentagon, I hear. Something about the Pentagon. Enough words and phrases emerge—"plane crash," "hijacked," "terror"—for me to understand that what's being said echoes the sketchy story we'd heard minutes before from a cop in front of the precinct house on our block. He, the cop, said that the Empire State Building was hit, then corrected himself. "No, it's the World Trade Center. The planes crashed into the World *Trade* Center." While he spoke, he smiled the soft, conspiratorial smile of someone delivering incredible news.

Though others in the crowd must be desperate for that news, for words to surround the torn-open towers rising into the silence, no one follows us over to the car. It's then I realize that the man, like many limo and taxi drivers in the city, might be from Pakistan. I glance his way again, but because he's leaning back against the seat, his chest and spread-wide legs are all I can see.

Fear slices through the shock. The burning towers have something to do with terror, and terror has to do with men like him.

The next moment I feel ashamed.

Chuck says, "Let's go."

It seems important to thank the man, and in this way apologize for my unspoken sin, but my husband is already walking away.

When I start to wheel the stroller after him, Gracie, who has been quiet till now, points at the limo's polished side, the glossy darkness that holds our bowed reflections, and shouts, "Car! Car!"

Civic Duty

Across the room are two voting booths with American flags decaled onto the sides. Four election officials sit behind card tables. Besides us, they're the only other people in the school gymnasium.

The election clerk's mouth moves. She seems to be asking me my name. Today is the primary election in New York. Chuck and I came out to vote, and now we're voting. We came out to vote, then turned the corner to see the World Trade Center on fire. Nothing seems particularly real.

"Tell me again," the clerk says. "I think I'm in shock. I'm terrified. Look at me, I'm trembling."

It hasn't yet occurred to me to feel frightened that way.

"There, I found you."

She points to my signature. A moment passes before I recognize the fast scrawl as mine.

After signing on the line next to it and being given a blue card with the number 46, I am directed to approach one of the booths. Behind the locked floor-to-ceiling cage next to it lie stacks of orange and blue exercise mats, which emit the musty-sharp smell I have come to associate with this civic duty.

"You know what to do, don't you?" asks the elderly man who takes the card away from me.

To be polite, I nod.

Pushing the curtain aside, I step in. Before me are a number of small metal levers with names beside them. Though I've voted in almost every election since turning eighteen, I'm at a loss. It's not that I've forgotten the steps, exactly; I'm just a little paralyzed. Eventually I press down the levers next to the names Green and Lopez. Other races wait for a decision, but I seem to have gone blank. Pulling the big red lever to the left, I make my limited choices irrevocable.

On the other side of the curtain, my daughter is arching her chest against the straps that bind her into the stroller, a small superhero in chains.

"There's Mommy, see?" my husband says.

Suddenly, a man's voice echoes from the ceiling. "Until further notice, no one may leave the building. Because of the situation, no one may leave. It is imperative . . ."

Searching for the voice's origin, the election clerk stares upward. Following her gaze, I notice that the long, blinding bars of fluorescent light are covered with the same metal grating that protects the gym mats from theft.

"They mean the kids. It's the *kids* who can't leave." Ever so slightly, her thin shoulders relax. "You know what?" she says. "As soon as I can, I'm out of here."

IN THE LIFE AFTER

Above and to the side of the towers is the word "Live." Whitely, it floats in the televised sky.

The same buildings a few minutes ago, in real life, were in sharper focus, but the extent of the damage is clearer on the screen. The second tower is in worse shape than I thought. Everything is worse than I thought.

My neighbor Elinor's nails press hard into my palms, almost but not quite breaking the skin. Holding hands, we sit on the couch staring at the set.

Watching the World Trade Center burn on TV doesn't make the fact more or less real, it just turns it into a story that envelopes us all.

The phone rings. I pull my hand from Elinor's and, balancing Gracie on one hip, answer.

It's my mother, calling from New Mexico.

"We're okay," I say into the receiver.

Sitting back down, I reposition the baby on my lap. Chuck is and isn't here, I tell her. He went up on the roof for a better look.

Remembering him, I glance out the window. Across the street, people stand in profile against the deep clear blue. The tops of the tenements are as crowded as they are on the Fourth of July, when fireworks explode over the East River.

"Look, sweetheart," I say absently to Gracie. "People."

"I see men!"

It's the baby. She has spoken—has shouted in delight—her first full English sentence. This watermark, which on any other day would have been met with joy, goes unnoticed till I remember much, much later.

"I see men!" Gracie shrieks again.

"And women, too," I murmur.

"What?" my mother says.

Suddenly the air fills with screams. Later I'll realize that they issued from those rooftop women and men, those neighbors and witnesses, but in this moment the howls seem to bleed from the sky.

On the screen, one tower has disappeared in a black cloud.

Elinor kneels on the carpet. Though she doesn't seem to be crying, her cheeks shine with tears. Someone—is it her?—is moaning. The sounds are the rhythmic grunts of a woman in labor.

My mother is telling the woman, telling me, "Try to be calm for the baby. Try. Try, honey, try."

SHOPPING

Not all of the lights are on inside. The cosmetics counter—the first thing we see when we enter the Kmart on Astor Place— is covered with white sheets molded to the mirrors and displays underneath. In the dimness, the department store looks like an abandoned ancestral home.

We're here because Gracie grew restless from being kept in all day under the eye of the TV. But when we got outside, the smoky air stung our cheeks and throats. I didn't want to— couldn't—think of what it was we were breathing. Going to the park was out of the question.

We ended up at Kmart because the bookstore that was our vague destination was closed. Most the stores were closed, as if for a national holiday. Few people could be seen. Except for the occasional emergency vehicle, the streets were empty of traffic. In the downtown sky hung a thick black plume of smoke, a frozen-still tornado. The afternoon light fell golden on the windows and walls.

Then we reached Lafayette Street. Filling the sidewalks on both sides of the wide avenue was a slow parade of people walking north. Ash dusted some of them. A man in green surgical scrubs bled from a butterfly-bandaged wound on his temple. Most of the others, though, wore business suits with the jackets missing or slung over one shoulder, as if they were returning home from a long day at work.

Beyond the cosmetics counter stand stacked cartons of Halloween candy. Miniature Milky Ways. Three Musketeers.

"Think it's open?" Chuck asks.

"Wouldn't they have locked the doors?"

None of the usual rules hold, though. Pushing the stroller, I walk deeper into the cavern, not knowing what we'll find.

No cashiers stand at the bank of counters. Behind the candy cartons is the only other customer, a middle-aged woman with several brightly colored garments draped over one arm. Without glancing our way, she turns toward women's sleepwear.

The air conditioning isn't on, but the escalator is running, its metal teeth rising into the semi-gloom. I unstrap Gracie. Chuck takes her hand, and together they step onto the moving stairway. Not wanting to lose sight of them for a second, I fold the stroller and follow.

At the top of the escalator are two white ghosts, one with a plastic jack-o'-lantern head. Still holding her father's hand, Gracie jumps happily up and down.

"What now?" Chuck asks.

"We let her play, I guess."

But she's already broken away from us and the white-sheeted manikins and has run down a shadowed aisle.

Trailing after her, I stop cold. Hundreds of shoes lie scattered on the floor. Pumps, work boots, slippers, and heels are piled high in mismatched mounds. The racks that usually hold them are bare.

Later I'll think of the photos of shoes from the death camps, the piles of moccasins from the slaughters here at home. But in this moment, the ability to make comparisons has left me. There is only the awful now.

Hugging a black boot to her chest, Gracie staggers around a corner, out of sight. Chuck strides after her.

When I find them again, she has abandoned the boot for a kitchen broom, the pink straw still wrapped in its plastic sheath.

"Clean!" she shouts.

Letting the stroller sag to the floor, I kneel before my daughter. "Give Mommy a hug." It's beginning to dawn on me why the shoes are strewn around as if the dark tornado outside had swept down through the aisles. The wingtips and high heels worn at work proved useless on the long walk to safety and home. Either that or shoes had been lost in the escape, the pandemonium. The walkers—those thousands of people who survived the destruction and fire—had been in need.

"Let's get out of here," Chuck says.

Gracie shakes her head no. She clasps the broom tighter.

UNIVERSAL DONOR (SEPTEMBER 12)

Sometime after one in the morning, we turn off the TV, fall asleep. When I awaken in the gray dawn, it's on again. As if no time has passed.

The words "Blood Line" flash onto the screen. Chuck writes the number in his notebook, then turns to me and says, "Is it okay if I'm gone for a while?"

His blood type is O negative, which makes him a universal donor. Though the idea of being apart from him unnerves me, I nod. We need to help.

He punches in the number, listens. After he sets down the receiver, I ask, "Are you going to Beth Israel or St. Vincent's?"

"Neither. They want us to call back tomorrow. My guess is they have enough."

Enough. I imagine the long lines of New Yorkers patiently waiting to open their veins for the survivors. The terrible mystery, though, is how few survivors have been found. The high estimate places fifty thousand people in the towers when the planes struck home. There must be—have to be—thousands trapped in the rubble, still alive.

POSTERITY (SEPTEMBER 12)

After leaning out the window to check for smoke, I dress Gracie, then head over to Tompkins Square Park.

Expecting to be one of the few parents insane enough to take a child into the smoldering world, I swing open the iron gate to find that the playground is full. In fact, the number of kids swells beyond what it can be on a sunny Saturday afternoon.

Children wearing shorts and summer dresses run across the shade-dappled asphalt. A boy a few months younger than

Gracie bumps his walker into her stroller. "Oopsy," I say. Head bent in concentration, he doesn't seem to notice.

Parental fears aside, the crowded playground makes a kind of sense. School has been suspended. The city has come to a standstill. Businesses and stores are closed, as are the universities where Chuck and I teach. The airports and subways have been shut down, traffic below Fourteenth Street, banned. We are in the cordoned-off zone that on the news is being called Ground Zero. There's not much else we can do.

I wheel Gracie over to the swings. *Ground Zero.* Something like war has descended on us. This is what it must be like to find yourself in a war zone while trying to live your life—a life that, if you're lucky, appears to go on as before.

Squatting near the circle of earth around an elm tree, Gracie watches Miles and Joaquin push yellow dump trucks through the dust. Jon, Reina, Karin, and Judy wave me over.

"How are you?" I ask.

"How are *you*?"

The question no longer is casual.

"All right, I guess."

"And Chuck?" Karin's eyes anxiously narrow, ready to resolve into an expression of pity or sorrow.

"He's fine."

He stayed home, I tell them, to watch the news. I don't tell them he's been at it all day. While I understand his need—it's mine, too—our separation feels like a wound. To be apart from him now leaves me aching in ways that have to do with survival.

I ask about Steve, a playground father who has a suit-and-tie job downtown. Wasn't his office in the World Trade Center?

"World *Financial* Center," Jon says. "Rei managed to reach Julie. He got out okay."

Holding his thumb and index finger inches apart, Jon says that friends in Brooklyn who called before the phone lines went dead told him that their yard was this deep in ashes and pieces of paper.

"They even found the pages of an emergency manual."

"An emergency manual?"

"Oh God."

"I can't believe—"

"None of it can be believed."

Jon is a musician, Reina a bartender, Karin an ESL teacher, and her partner, Judy, a screenwriter. Like most of the parents I know from this Avenue A playground, they have what can be called unconventional jobs. Steve is the only one stationed in the Financial District. The rest of us are writers, performers, artists of some kind. We work in publishing, fashion, or film, wait tables, design, teach. On the face of it, few of us have been directly touched by the disaster.

The out-of-state relatives and friends who managed to get through to us believed otherwise, believed that we might have been in danger. I reassured them. Our days' orbit, I said, is defined by work and the playground and home. Chuck and I rarely find ourselves far from our apartment, and in this we're not alone. New York isn't really a city, I said, it's a thousand small towns crammed together into the idea of a city.

"Don't worry, we're almost a mile and a half from the World Trade Center," I told them, translating the blocks into terms non–New Yorkers could understand.

A mile and a half, I realized as I spoke, wasn't that great a distance. A mile and a half away, the wreckage burns. A mile and a half away, people lie crushed and dying and dead. Smoke hangs in the south. Sirens softly wail. We stand at Ground Zero with our children scattered around us.

Tucked under Jon's arm is a *Daily News* he must have walked north of the Fourteenth Street blockades to buy.

"Want a look?" he asks.

Thumbing through the tabloid sheets, I see, in black and white, the burning towers, the falling towers, people whose faces are ashen masks.

Then I come to the photo of the severed hand. A length of bone extrudes from the wrist. The fingers curl so that they point from the debris-littered street straight up at me.

Without thinking, I fold the pages back, in the manner of commuters on rush-hour trains.

"Careful," says Jon. "I'm saving it for posterity."

PRAYER (SEPTEMBER 13)

During the night, the wind changed direction. Haze films the morning sky. Yellow clouds drift over the projects across First

Avenue. Though we've closed all the windows, the burned-plastic odor still seeps through.

When the wind finally shifts to the east, Chuck and I decide to take Gracie for a walk. Near the police station are two men with white particle masks over their noses and mouths. The woman a few steps behind them wears a red scarf tied bandit style around her face. Second Avenue is almost deserted. No traffic. The handful of people we see are wearing masks, as if the city had been swept by plague.

Aware of the nakedness of our faces—of Gracie's face—I realize that we're in a kind of hell. With each revolution of the stroller's wheels, I'm pushing our daughter deeper into it.

The doors to the Middle Collegiate Church stand open. After Gracie was born, we began to worship there, though "worship" may be too strong a word for what I do. This ecumenical Protestant church welcomes people like us, who are ambivalent about organized religion but feel the need for prayer.

One of the ministers, Jeanne, beckons us inside. She's wearing a sleeveless dress the deep purple-blue of irises. They've kept the church open as a refuge, she tells us. Before we enter she hands us three particle masks. "In case you need them later," she says.

Cool air surrounds us. The bitter smell that's everywhere hasn't penetrated the sanctuary.

Beneath the altar burns a single white candle.

"I'll take the baby," Chuck says.

While Gracie runs through the pews, I close my eyes, then lay my head on folded arms. My eyelids twitch. TV images from the past three days replay in fast succession. Tiny blurs that are people fall past the gleaming façade. The North Tower waterfalls in on itself. The world is covered with ashes.

I'm sobbing. My shoulders heave, but even in the fullness of grief I understand that crying here is different from crying at home. I have become a woman weeping in a church, one of countless women who have wept in churches through the ages. One of many. A single mote.

Something like quietness comes over me, and then I feel them. The air is raked with the presence of the people who've died and are dying. *I know you're here,* I want to say.

Finding a tissue, I blow my nose, stand up. Two other women are now seated in the pews behind me. The baby's running feet thud on the carpet. I go to my husband. It's time to relieve of him of Gracie duty so that so he, too, may have the chance to pray.

Helping (September 13)

On the sidewalk outside the church we run into Vicki, a mother I know from the park. Her son, Aaron, isn't with her. Hugely pregnant with her second child, she wears a particle mask, which she pulls down under her chin when she sees us.

"Aren't you due any day?" I ask.

"This weekend."

Laying a hand on her belly, Vicki smiles, and I half enviously remember the feeling of peace that cushioned me when I was pregnant.

Thinking about her soon-to-be-born baby, I wonder what she's doing outside in all of this.

As if she can read my mind, she says, "I went over to St. Vincent's to see if they needed help."

She's a doctor, a family practitioner.

"Did they?"

"No and yes."

The few injured survivors were easily treated by the physicians on staff, so there was nothing for her or the scores of other doctor-volunteers to do.

"Except listen," she says.

Listen?

The hospital was packed with people searching for lost relatives, lovers, friends. "They needed to talk, so I listened. I listened for hours."

Talking might ease the pain, but words could be lifelines, too. If the story got out, a miracle might occur. The comatose brother or mother might be identified, the amnesiac wandering the streets, found and brought safely home.

Were there any miracles? I ask.

No.

Her eyes go dim. Stories change the listener, and I wonder if she's thinking about all the desperate ones she heard. But then I remember how prebirth contractions alone are enough to cloud your eyes. That sensation of being in the body's grip, of feeling that the inevitable is almost here.

SANCTUARY (SEPTEMBER 13)

On the restaurant walls hang a series of semi-abstract paintings of New York. All major landmarks are represented. The Brooklyn Bridge. The Empire State Building. The World Trade Center towers are two blue roads in the sky.

We're the only customers at Kiev. Restless in her high chair, Gracie refuses to touch her blintzes and pea soup. None of us are hungry. I'm not sure why I insisted we come, other than out of a thin conviction that daily rituals, like eating lunch, must be observed.

The city beyond the windows is haunted, the quiet broken only by faraway sirens and the slicing roar of an occasional F-16. All the usual noise is gone. No delivery trucks, buses, or cabs crowd the avenue. No subways rumble underground. No passenger planes leave crisscrossed vapor trails above. Without the steady hum rising from the narrow island we call home, I can't believe anything really exists.

The young waiter plays peek-a-boo with Gracie. "She reminds me of my little sister," he says.

When we leave, he stands in the doorway waving good-bye.

Suddenly, dense yellow clouds pour down Second Avenue. Within seconds we're wrapped in a stinging fog.

I fumble in the diaper bag for a particle mask, but when I press the white cup over Gracie's face, she twists her head away. I press harder. Eyes wide with hurt surprise, she starts to cry.

Snatching my daughter from the stroller, I run across the street. The doors of the church are still open. Jeanne and the head minister, Gordon, stand just inside.

Folding the stroller, Chuck asks if we can stay till the air clears.

"Of course," Gordon says. He adds that if Gracie likes, she can play in the community room behind the sanctuary.

A standing fan slowly rotates before the barred window. The high-ceilinged room is bright with natural light. Gracie laughs, then takes off, running.

After a while, Jeanne comes in and sits on the edge of the wooden stage. The purple sheath she's wearing glows with the slight shimmer of linen or raw silk.

"That's a lovely dress," I tell her.

"I thought people might like to see some color instead of black."

Chuck opens the double doors to the nursery, where the youngest kids play during Sunday services. Finding a pull toy shaped like a dachshund, he hands the string to Gracie.

An idea forms, and before I can fully think it out, I ask Jeanne if we can invite over some friends with small children. The kids have been cooped up, I explain, and need a safe place to play.

I make the calls on Jeanne's cell phone. Soon the families arrive. Dublin, Adeola, Jack, and Gracie run barefoot across the tiled floor; the parents sit with Jeanne quietly talking and eating the chocolates Sharon brought. For the first time since the towers fell, happiness seems possible.

About an hour later, Gordon walks in. Glancing at our sweaty toddlers he says, "I would put shoes on them. A lot of people have come through in the past few days, and we haven't had a chance to clean."

With him is a young man whose clothes are gray with ashes. A paisley bandana covers his hair; his skin has the reddened hue of white people who live on the street. He's saying something, his voice low, urgent, fast. Nodding vague assent, Gordon steers him toward a table in the corner, then disappears. Returning with a paper plate of crackers and cheese, he says, "This is about all we have left."

The man anxiously eyes the food but does not yet eat. "Basically, I've been homeless since it happened," he says. There's the whole story to be got through, about the smoke and dust and wandering around in shock.

Finished, he bows his head as if in prayer. "To tell the truth," he says, "I never really had a home."

Hypothetical Dangers (September 13)

"No, sweetie, don't stand so close to the TV. It's bad for you."

Wearing only a diaper, Gracie dances on the carpet two feet from the screen. The way she dances is to bounce up and down and wave her arms in imitation of the monsters in *Where the Wild Things Are.*

Rising from the couch, I kneel behind her. Again the fire-ball bursts through the South Tower, as if the steel and glass and people inside were as insubstantial as air.

"I'm going to help you move," I murmur in her ear.

Her dark-blonde hair is drenched with sweat. We've closed the windows against the smoke and kept the air conditioning off, afraid of asbestos and other toxins blowing through the vents. Lifting Gracie's damp body, I think of the fibers that even now might be lodged in her lungs. My daughter bears the seeds of her death inside her—if not from the airborne carcinogens all around us, then from some other source. My chest tightens. Why haven't I done more to keep her safe?

The next moment, I'm ashamed of my selfishness. I have no right to worry about my own family, no right to dwell on hypothetical dangers. Not when so many people have died.

Gracie twists out of my arms. Standing again, she raises both arms over her head. Her eyes gleam with maniacal light.

"Boom!" she shouts. "Boom! Plane!"

THE NEWS (SEPTEMBER 13)

No, says the man whose unsmiling face fills the screen. No, the sporadic gunfire heard beneath the rubble can't possibly be signals from trapped police officers calling for help. No, it's likely that the immense heat generated by the underground blaze caused their service revolvers to spontaneously fire.

"You're saying the guns are going off all by themselves?" a man's voice asks.

"Yes, that's correct. All by themselves."

RAIN (SEPTEMBER 14)

Lightning flashed across the sky. Thunder boomed. I stirred awake and, in a thought that was half idea and half dream, told myself *storm*. Further on in the night, I woke up again and thought the words *We're all going to die*. Holding on to Gracie, I fell back to sleep.

This morning it's still raining. Chuck turns on the TV. The weather will hamper rescue efforts, the anchorman says.

Rescue efforts. Since Tuesday, the day of the attack, only four people have been pulled from the rubble alive. Among the confirmed dead are eight children.

The same rain slashing the window washes dust and blood down the gutters, out to the rivers and sea.

THE ACQUISITION OF LANGUAGE (SEPTEMBER 14)

Gathering words to herself like shiny new toys, Gracie has learned to say "Allah," "Taliban," and "Kabul."

While she plays with her plastic farm animals, I stare at the TV. For the first time I notice that the faint vertical bar of fuzz that usually divides the screen is gone. Interference from the World Trade towers is no more.

Billy Graham is on. His lips move, creating words that I can't seem to string into sentences. An imam preaches next, followed by an African American minister. Though I'm having trouble understanding what they're saying, tears drip from my chin onto my knees.

Gracie stops playing to solemnly watch me. Managing a smile, I tell her I'm sad but that everything's okay. It's all right for mommies to be sad now and then.

The camera pans the National Cathedral. Some sitting in the pews dab their faces. I'm grateful to be too upset to hear the sermon because I'm in no shape to absorb another message. The official messages so far have to do with striking back, and the idea of more death hurts me. This empathy is powerful, new. The pain feels physical, almost as real as a fist driven between the ribs.

Pointing at a sobbing woman, Gracie says, "People sad." Turning to me, she adds, "Mommy sad."

I lift her onto my lap. "Are you sad, honey?"

"Bu zhidao."

In the Mandarin Gracie is learning from family friends, her baby-sitter, Ping, and, to a much lesser extent, me, *bu zhidao* means "I don't know." It's what she says whenever she wants to be told a thing's name.

SLEEP (SEPTEMBER 14)

Suddenly I'm so tired I sleep whenever I can.

In the hot afternoon, curled around my daughter's

drowsing warmth, I startle awake. Without the mercy of a second or two of forgetfulness, the memory of what happened comes back.

SCARCITY (SEPTEMBER 14)

We decide to order pizza for supper.

"Peppers and onions?" Chuck asks, reaching for the basket of takeout menus.

"Sure."

A couple of minutes later, he leans into the living room, where I'm playing roll-the-ball with Gracie. His hand is cupped over the receiver.

"No peppers," he says. "Want meatballs instead?"

"Meatballs are fine."

No one runs out of anything in New York, I think, not if they have the money. But since Tuesday, delivery trucks, along with all other non-emergency traffic, have been barred from Lower Manhattan. Our neighborhood is an island within an island, under quarantine, infected by death.

Chuck disappears, then leans back into sight, hand again held over the receiver.

"No meatballs either."

"Olives?"

"Do you have olives?"

Listening, he shakes his head no.

"Onions is all?" His eyes meet mine. "Then onions it is."

HEALING (SEPTEMBER 14)

The last time we were here, a single candle burned before the
altar. Now a whole bank of candles flickers at the front of the
crowded church.

Liselot, Adeola's mother, gives me a sorrowful look.

"How are you?" I ask.

"Not so good."

Holding Gracie, I slide into the pew next to Liselot and her
daughter. Carrying the diaper bag, Chuck squeezes in with us.
Though I don't tell my friend, I'm shaken by her answer. I'm
not so good either, but if I admit it I might fall apart. *Going to
pieces*, I hear my mother's voice say. I might go to pieces.

Adeola's small face dimples into a smile. Gracie happily
wiggles in greeting, then scrambles out into the aisle.

"No, sweetie, sit. You can sit next to Ola."

But Adeola has squirmed past our knees and is standing in
the aisle, too. Liselot and I end up trailing the girls around
the packed sanctuary. The service begins. I'm unsure of the
agenda but think we're here to pray for the dead, to pray for
peace. Gordon, though, is saying something about healing.

Anger rises, tingling at my throat, and I realize I don't want
to heal, can't heal, can't hear a word about it yet. Not while the
tip of the island on which we stand is a smoldering wound.

"Let's go into the back," Liselot whispers.

The doors to the community room swing open on to a
half-lit metal-and-veneer forest of tables and folding chairs. A
young man wearing a white do-rag sits on one of the chairs.

On his lap is a girl who's about a year old. The golden balls lodged in her earlobes gleam.

"What do you say, Ola?" he says.

Liselot greets him warmly, then tells me that Abdul helps look after the children during the services. The girl with him is his niece, Glory.

As if loath to hear herself discussed, Glory slips from Abdul's lap and strides off between the tables. Gracie and Adeola follow her.

"She walks so well," I tell him.

I'm glad to be distracted by the kids. *Healing.* We have to mourn first, but the problem is, I'm not sure how to begin. How can I mourn? What right do I have? To my knowledge, nobody I know was killed in the attacks. My unfocused grief seems selfish, disrespectful to those who lost loved ones in the towers and the Pentagon and Pennsylvania fields.

When we reenter the sanctuary, the congregation is filing out through the front doors. Almost everyone holds candles, slim white tapers with cardboard collars to catch the molten drops.

"I was about to come get you," Chuck says. He hands Liselot and me two unlit candles, then gives Gracie a hug.

Since we're among the last to leave, we wind up standing on the top steps next to Gordon, who's now talking about letting the light of peace be seen. Chuck touches his candle to mine. The waxed string hisses, ignites. I think about the fire burning to the south and wonder how fire and its terrible power can ever stand for peace.

Gracie, in my arms, reaches out to touch the flame.

"No, honey! It's hot!" I whisper.

Fanning down the stairs and out onto the sidewalk and avenue beyond are hundreds of people, all holding candles. Together, our lights form a small galaxy.

NOTHING IN THE WORLD (SEPTEMBER 15)

Jordan's mother, Ella, gives his swing another push. While she talks, she effortlessly keeps up the rhythm, hands meeting the swing back's hard rubber without her having to look.

Ella is a fashion designer who works in Tribeca. She's telling me how, after the second plane hit, she frantically dialed home, only to learn that the baby had just gone out with his sitter.

"That was the most awful part—not knowing where he was."

The muscles in her long, thin arms flex with each push. When the first tower fell, she left the studio, then found herself among the thousands of people running up Broadway.

What did she do?

"What else could I do? Run with them."

Staring at his mother, Jordan reaches out his arms. Without breaking the flow of her story, Ella lifts him out of the black bucket. Now that their faces are side by side, I see that their eyes are the same startling shade of blue.

"A couple of nights ago, when the thunder started, I woke up screaming." She walks toward the gate. Raising the iron latch, she says, "My husband couldn't stop me. Nothing in the world could have stopped me."

Fear of Heights (September 15)

The bowl of fruit on Breyten and Yolande's table looks like part of an eighteenth-century French still life.

Gracie reaches for a grape.

"Can she have some?" I ask.

Yolande smiles. "Of course."

Though the tableau is too perfect to disturb, she breaks off a stem. But before she can hand it to my daughter, I intercede. Grapes are choking food. Popping one in my mouth, I bite down. Only after I've chewed the purple globe into safe-to-swallow bits do I offer it.

While fond of our hosts, I hadn't wanted to come out to dinner with them. Yolande and Breyten are staying for the semester in a faculty high-rise in the West Village just north of Houston Street, several blocks closer than we are to the World Trade Center. The thought of taking Gracie any nearer the burning ruins and floodlit clouds made me uneasy. The awful work going on under those clouds no longer goes by the name of "rescue." The new word is "recovery."

Breyten hands me a glass of red wine, then leans back against the radiator cover that runs the length of the picture window.

The window looks out on a high-rise identical to theirs. From an upper balcony hangs a peace sign painted on what looks like a bed sheet. The skeleton of the under-construction student center looms nearby.

Breyten is in the middle of telling Chuck and Russell the story of what he saw on Tuesday morning. He was on the balcony writing when he heard a roar, followed by a loud boom. Looking down, he noticed a group of construction workers facing south, pointing. Thinking the explosion signaled an accident, he went to the other side of the building to investigate and saw the North Tower in flames.

The door to the balcony stands open. As if lured by Breyten's words, Gracie swaggers through it. I rush after her. Twelve stories below lie the complex's sidewalks, arranged in pale loops. I gasp. My mild fear of heights has suddenly blossomed into terror.

"Let's go back inside," I say.

After nudging Gracie to safety, I close the door. Breyten eyes me—wryly, I think—then turns back to the conversation.

They're now talking about how the language has been co-opted by those in power, with aid from an unquestioning media. Phrases like "America's New War" and "Operation Noble Eagle" not only obscure insidious militaristic intent but take possession of the words' meaning. They're no longer ours, can no longer be used as we would use them. They have been stolen. Take the word "freedom," for instance. What can it possibly signify now that it's become shorthand for "war"?

Wanting to hear more, I angle closer to the radiator, but Gracie is heading back toward the table and the alluring bowl of choking fruit. I have no choice but to follow. The apartment is too fraught with danger—exposed sockets, extension cords, paper clips, bowls of peanuts, glasses of wine—for my attention to waver for a second.

When Gracie toddles past Breyten's knees, he grins, then lifts her onto the radiator cover beside him. She stands, presses her face and hands against the glass.

Its transparency is the only thing separating her from the sky.

A SMALL TOWN LIKE ME (SEPTEMBER 16)

Under the white tents sit baskets of apples, loaves of bread. Today is the second day that the city south of Fourteenth Street has been reopened to traffic, but I'm still surprised to see the trucks and folding tables of the farmer's market at Tompkins Square Park. As if this were any Saturday in September.

The Blueberry Man tucks a plastic-mesh basket of fruit into a paper bag. Voice tinged with urgency, he's talking to a woman who holds four dollar bills splayed before her like playing cards.

Done bagging the berries, he gestures at the sidewalk beside us. All three of us—he, the woman, and I—glance at the interlocked gray paving stones.

"They're Pakistani," he says, and I realize he means the

Muslim couple who sell organic vegetables. Their cucumbers and rainbow chard are the best the market has to offer, the flesh of the cukes crisp and sweet, the chard leaves tender, not too large. Most of the time I deal with the woman, who remembers me and chats about the weather and growing season. I see the head scarf circling her face, her hands lifting a bunch of beets from the scale.

Neither she nor her husband is here. The stretch of sidewalk allocated to their stand is empty.

The Blueberry Man now holds a cell phone. Each pressed number is a soft atonal beep.

"They live in a small town, like me, where everyone's white," he says. "I'm calling to see if they're okay."

In the Playground (September 16)

Seated at the top of the metal slide, Gracie holds on to the rails to keep herself from plummeting down.

The descent, I realize, must seem endless.

"Come on, honey, Mommy will catch you."

A boy who might be two years old—I search for but can't remember his name—stands behind her. With a sandaled foot he gently prods her plump behind.

"Let's go, sweetheart. There's someone waiting."

Gracie shakes her head no. Her eyes are grave. Though she's working hard to fight her fear, I'm beginning to grow impatient.

"Then you'll have to move so the boy can have a turn."

His father appears on the other side of the slide's steel tongue. "That's all right," he says. "Buddy, let's find something else to do. Want to climb the monkey bars?"

"Sorry," I tell him.

"For what?"

I can't remember his name either, but we've talked several times before. Once, when his son bumped his head, I lent him the ice pack from Gracie's lunch bag to ease the swelling.

Together we watch his boy scale a green ladder.

"How are you?" I ask.

He shakes his head. "Pretty terrible."

I wait for him to talk about the lost relative or friend, but instead he looks right at me and says, "I can't stand what's going on in Afghanistan. I don't want us to spend a dime to kill anyone else."

Relieved, I nod in agreement. The relief comes from knowing that others feel the wound of violence. I can tell by his voice that for him, too, the revulsion is more than moral. Bombs shatter earth, blast flesh to dust. The idea of people being killed fills me with the same clean pain that invades every time I think of the thousands crushed to dust. The deaths so near have made the world's other deaths real.

Gracie lets go of her hold and, with a yelp of fear or joy, flies down.

VERY SCARY (SEPTEMBER 16)

The young woman seated across the kitchen table has lived in New York for exactly eleven days. Humera is a graduate student of Chuck's. Her studio apartment in Soho is less than a mile from the leveled World Trade Center.

"This is delicious," she politely says.

Taking another small bite of pasta, she wipes her mouth on the folded paper towel that serves as a napkin. She hasn't eaten a home-cooked meal since the attack, she tells us, because she was afraid to walk beyond the cordons to a supermarket. You had to show an ID to get back in, and because she's a Pakistani national she was worried about being able to return.

For the first two days, she sat in her apartment listening to the radio. The farthest she dared go was the deli on the corner. When she finally went to a café for dinner, she heard a couple of men at the next table talking about "those fucking Arabs."

"So I leaned down and, as discreetly as I could, took out my nose ring."

Glancing at Humera's lovely face, I see no sign of the ring or piercing. She's wearing jeans and a blue blouse. With her high cheekbones and dark copper hair, she could easily be Italian, Latina, American Indian, or, like me, half Chinese. In New York, nose ring or not, she could be practically anything.

"I'm sorry it's been so hard," I say.

Humera lays down her fork. The stories come flooding out. Friends across the country keep calling with news of violence that goes unreported by the media. Chuck and I have read about the murdered Sikh convenience store clerk in Arizona and the veiled woman on Long Island who was chased through a shopping mall by a white man yelling, "I've got to kill her!" an assault no one moved to stop. Now Humera tells us about the friend of a friend in San Francisco who was stabbed on his way home from mosque, about the two Muslim girls in Boston gang-raped by sixteen men.

"Do you mind if we watch the news?" she asks. The destruction of the towers knocked out all non-satellite reception, she apologetically explains, so her TV only gets snow.

We sit on the couch drinking tea while a plane explodes through the bright glass. Humera doesn't speak for a while. Finally she says, "This is the first time I've seen the images."

When the news segments begin to loop, Chuck goes to the bookcase where the videotapes are kept.

"Every fiction writer should take a look at this," he says, and slips Akira Kurosawa's *Dreams* into the VCR.

Tired of the disaster footage—for the past half hour she's tugged at my hair and tried to get Humera to play peek-a-boo—Gracie raptly watches a boy in a blue kimono walk through the forest. Out of the mist comes a solemn procession of fox spirits. Though the actors' makeup is deliberately artificial in a way more suggestive of the stage than the screen, the effect is magical.

A couple of dream segments later, the screen darkens. Mountain climbers are trapped in a blizzard. Snowflakes glitter like flecks of mica caught in a flashlight's beam. The frozen men slowly trudge through the snow, then collapse in the deep, ashen drifts.

When the leader opens his eyes, a woman in a fluttering robe is covering him with a silver shawl. She's whispering, her voice electric and low. The golden words at the bottom of the screen read, "The snow is warm, the ice is hot."

She could be a kind of angel, but something isn't right. When the man tries to rise, she gently presses his chest until he sinks back into the snow. The wind whips the long hair away from her face, revealing the black-lined eyes of a demon.

"Very scary," Gracie says.

Tears run down her cheeks.

Humera looks at her, then at Chuck and me. I grab the remote, hit stop, fast forward. Not for the first time do I wonder what our daughter makes of the apparitions moving across the screen.

Pulling her onto my lap, I say, "Yes, sweetie, it *is* scary. But it's pretend, not real. Mommy and Daddy and Humera are here. Everything is fine."

The News (September 16)

The anchorwoman says relatives of the missing are urged to bring DNA samples to the National Guard Armory, which is serving as a morgue.

"DNA samples?"

Hairbrushes, the anchorwoman says. Toothbrushes, electric razors. Underwear.

"Underwear," Chuck echoes. "Jesus."

Neither of us has to utter a word. I try—and fail—to block out the scene of the not-to-be-written story that crowds the air around us.

The woman, because most of them would be women, digs through the laundry basket. Finding the pair of green jockey shorts he wore for good luck, she lifts them to her face and breathes. A black T-shirt is also infused with his scent. Turning off the light, she strips, then lies down on the bed. She carefully arranges the shirt over her chest, the shorts over her groin.

When that doesn't bring him back, she finds the ridge where the T-shirt's sleeve is sewn on to the torso. Taking the cloth into her mouth, she sucks on it, drawing what's left of his essence into her body.

LOVE OF COUNTRY (SEPTEMBER 16)

For the first five nights after the attack, the Empire State Building was kept dark, the floodlights that bathe its limestone walls turned off. A few scattered lights from office windows pocked its surface like stars. The red beacon on its spire flashed a warning to low-flying planes.

The remaining skyscrapers—the Chrysler and Citicorp buildings, and others I can't name—dimmed their lights in mourning, too.

With the bright clouds of disaster to the south and darkness to the north, the city at night was a city I no longer recognized. From our bedroom window, the Midtown skyline was a range of gray stalagmites. When I sat looking out at it after my family had gone to sleep, desolation was a stone in my chest. Sometimes I cried, softly so as not to wake Chuck or the baby.

Tonight, though, the Empire State Building is washed in light. Instead of its usual plain white, the skyscraper is dyed red, white, and blue.

With all the talk of retribution, bombing Afghanistan, going after bin Laden, the colors mean war.

I begin to weep.

I'm crying, I realize, for my country. I am flooded with love for America, not the America declaring war but the America hidden within the shell of the nation that surrounds it. My love is deeper than pledge-of-allegiance loyalty, deep enough to have survived decades of shame. Deep enough to survive whatever will come.

The hollow at the base of my throat aches with a searing, sad love of country so strong I must have had it in me all along.

THE NEXT ELEVEN DAYS

MORE LIKE HIROSHIMA (SEPTEMBER 17)

"No," says Christine, a student in my Asian American Lit class, "it wasn't like Pearl Harbor at all. Pearl Harbor was a military target, right?"

When she pushes a wing of black hair away from her face, the strands fall into place like hair in a shampoo ad. It's our first day back at school. Some students evacuated from the dormitory on Williams Street, three blocks from the World Trade Center, have been sleeping in the classrooms, maybe the very classroom where we sit in a circle of chairs. Christine is among the displaced. "It's not so bad," she told me before class began. "Really, I'm fine."

Now she's saying, "It was more like Hiroshima. We didn't give them any warning either, did we?"

Staring at her, I can't remember. I know that I know the answer, have known it for most of my life. I also recall that I've read several books on the subject of the first nuclear bombs, including *The Making of the Atomic Bomb*, Richard Rhodes's careful chronology of who knew what when.

But my memory has frozen over. Somewhere beneath the icy surface of the moment all I know lies half alive, intact but beyond reach.

Christine and the others are watching me. Waiting.

"Does anyone have the answer?" I say at last.

DEAD AIR (SEPTEMBER 17)

Dark smoke fills the screen. Smoke, though, isn't the right word for the debris clouding the air, collecting like sand on the video camera's lens. It's far too corporeal. This smoke is to real smoke as the ashes of a cremated body, heavy with silver flecks and bone chips, are to ashes, the powder-fine ones we're supposed to return to.

Seconds pass. There's a low roar, like crashing waves heard by someone dragged underwater. The darkness continues.

I don't think I've ever witnessed so much dead air, the newscasters' phrase for those accidental moments when the screen remains blank.

Finally the blackness clears. The street and everything on it—cars, signs, buildings, people—are covered in soft gray. The air is gray, too, as if storm clouds blocked the sun.

A man's voice says, "People need help. I don't think I'm one of them."

He starts to walk, taking shaky footage of the gray wasteland

and groups of gray firemen who stand around in motionless tableaus. His footsteps crunch, but otherwise the scene is silent. No, the silence isn't total. A chirping sound begins. It seems to issue from everywhere, like crickets chirring in the dark gold of late-summer country dusk.

The footage ends. Now on the screen is some kind of expert talking about what we've just seen. I half listen until he begins to explain the origin of the mysterious music. All firefighters, he says, are equipped with alarms that go off if the wearers lie still for more than a minute.

It takes me a second to understand.

Each sweet note signals a man buried beneath the rubble. A man who, moments before, was still alive.

SHRINES (SEPTEMBER 18)

Today the wind is carrying the smoke west across the Hudson. It seems safe to take Gracie outside.

Trying to ease her to sleep, I push the stroller through Tompkins Square Park. As it has for days, the air tastes like burned plastic and wire, but the sky is an unmarred blue. The weather has been gorgeous. I don't remember ever seeing the city look so beautiful. It must be the dust motes that deepen the light, glazing everything with fairy-tale gold.

We reach the circle where the park's band shell once stood. Beneath the two tall trees that used to shade concert audiences, peach-robed Krishna devotees often chant and dance. Today, though, the place is empty of people. In the space where the dancers usually swirl are flowers and votive candles with images of Jesus, Buddha, Krishna, Mary. A few of them still burn. Little rivers of wax trap the flower petals and leaves in their path.

In colored chalk—the same kind Gracie and her friends draw with on the sidewalk—someone has scratched a list of the types of rescue workers who died when the towers collapsed. Port Authority. Police. NYFD.

Block print in another hand reads

REMEMBER WHAT IS IMPORTANT

FAMILY FRIENDS LOVE

Enclosed within a small violet square are the words

May Our Sorrow
Be Tempered
By Reason

Gracie kicks at the stroller's foot rest, which in the past couple of weeks she's grown tall enough to reach. Fighting sleep, she struggles to sit up and see what's been occupying my attention.

"Colors!" she calls. "Oh, look!"

LIFE AND DEATH (SEPTEMBER 20)

So many votive candles sit before the hospital that, when we walk past, their heat wafts up at us. Behind them, the wall is plastered with fliers of those lost in the attack.

Missing persons. At what moment did the missing became the dead?

The rain that has been threatening all day begins to fall. We're here at St. Vincent's to visit our friend Jane and the new baby, who was born yesterday. When we find them, Jane has the small, blanketed bundle that's her second daughter pressed to her chest. Her eyes shine. She hasn't slept, she tells us, since going into labor the day before.

Her bed is by the window, which faces south. While we talk—about the birth, the new life in her arms—I can't help glancing outside. The rain is coming down hard now. The sky above the West Village is gray with it.

"Is that the smoke plume?" I ask.

Chuck stands to get a better look. Jane can't really move because of the nursing baby, but she cranes her neck to see.

After a moment Chuck says, "Impossible to tell with this weather."

"Maybe the storm will help put out the fire," says Jane.

I don't say aloud what I've heard on the news, that the fire burns too fiercely, too deeply, to be dampened by a little rain.

Smiling, Jane says, "Do you want to hold her?"

The warm bundle is impossibly light. I stare at the tiny face inside. The flesh around her almost-closed eyes looks bruised. Scratches furrow her scalp. The battle to be born was a hard one.

Back outside in the downpour, most of the votive candles have gone out. Two men are peeling rain-streaked fliers off the wall. Another man is hanging them up again, in neat rows, on a second wall beneath a cavelike overhang. Within the shadowed cave are lines of folding tables that have been laid with coffee urns, boxes of doughnuts, and cellophane-wrapped sandwiches. At the moment, there are no takers.

Across the street, the wall of what appears to be a restaurant is entirely covered with fliers. Sharing an umbrella, Chuck and I study them. Each sheet bears Xeroxed photos, most in color but some in black and white, of men and women who gaze out at us from specific moments in their lives. A wedding, graduation, Christmas. A day at the beach. Information follows, dates of birth, identifying marks. A tattoo of a scorpion on his right calf. A caesarean scar. A gold ring inscribed with the date 8/2/93.

We have to read every one.

"Please help me find my wife," one flier reads. "She worked on the 92nd floor of the South Tower. She is four months pregnant."

Chuck shudders, pulls me close.

After we're done, we begin the walk home. The phone kiosk on the corner has three fliers taped to one Plexiglas side.

The rain has already washed away most of the color, leaving the outlines of the bodies and faces behind.

A REAL POSSIBILITY (SEPTEMBER 21)

On the news is a story about the potential use of anthrax and smallpox as biological weapons.

"It is time to acknowledge bioterrorism as a real possibility," the anchor says.

"Bioterrorism?" I murmur.

Chuck leans forward to scoop more frozen yogurt into his bowl. "The fear is getting worse, isn't it?" he says.

I wonder if I'm susceptible to this fear. Since the day of the attacks on the World Trade Center and the Pentagon, I've grown heart-racingly afraid of heights and low-flying planes. More reasonably, I'm afraid of the toxic smoke we're all breathing.

Taking my emotional pulse, I realize I'm undisturbed by the latest theoretical threat.

Later that night, lying in bed, the baby's heels wedged against my rib cage, I understand why I'm not fazed by the idea of bioterrorism. I already *am* afraid. That death can come in a second isn't a lesson I need to learn twice.

TRIAGE (SEPTEMBER 24)

I thought I was over the first wave of shock, when tears brimmed to the surface before I even knew I was crying.

But on my way to the pool at the Y, it happens again. What
sets off the weeping this time is the sight of the man kneeling
before the fire station on Fourteenth Street. Like me, he's in
his forties. The short-sleeved yellow shirt he's wearing reveals
muscular arms.

The reason this powerful man is on his knees is so he can
pick the dry, wilted flowers from the bouquets that flank the
station house's entryway. As I walk by, he takes a mound of
dead blossoms in his arms, then carefully slides it into a black
plastic bag.

Turning his attention to the flowers that remain, he makes
new arrangements out of the surviving blooms.

COMPARED TO VIETNAM (SEPTEMBER 24)

Every time I greet one of my colleagues I ask, after it has been
established that no one he or she knew died on September 11,
"So how are classes going?"

The question is received as code for, How are your students
reacting to the horror? How are they making room for it
inside their lives? More to the point, how are *you* handling the
roil of emotions—the depression, anger, fear, zeal, and tears—
that seems to have become the curriculum?

At the faculty mailboxes I encounter Thinh. Every
Christmas Thinh gives us a basket of apple or pumpkin tarts
she has baked herself. All I know about Thinh's past is that
when she was twelve, she and her mother and sisters boarded

one of the last helicopters to leave Saigon in 1975. About Thinh's father and possible brothers I know nothing. Afraid of the answer, I've never asked.

"Classes are going great," Thinh says. She's wearing a light blue silk blouse. When she reaches for the papers that have collected in her box, I notice the slim crescent of a sweat stain under her arm. The tarts Thinh makes are covered with tiny dough maple leaves that have been brushed with sugared egg white, then baked to a glassy sheen. She is very slender, with the quick, calm reflexes of a trained athlete.

"What are they saying about the disaster?" I ask.

"Nothing. Nothing at all. They don't want to. They want to do what they came here to do."

Her smile has grown insistent, sharp.

"I don't know what all the fuss is about," she says. "Compared to Vietnam, this is nothing."

No One Else to Help (September 26)

Gripping a piece of blue chalk, Gracie draws three parallel lines on the pavement, then straightens up to admire her work.

"Nice job, sweetie," I say.

Next to her sits Winslow, who's three or four weeks older than she is.

"What are you going to draw this time, Win?" Bryce asks her son.

"A helicopter."

With green chalk the color of new grass, Winslow swiftly sketches a box with an X on top.

"Jesus," I murmur. "That actually looks like a helicopter."

"He draws all day long. Doesn't want to do anything else."

It turns out that Winslow already can write all the letters of the alphabet, too.

"Mr. Symbol," Bryce says.

"Amazing."

Because this is the first time I've seen Bryce since September 11, I ask how it was for them. They live somewhere below Canal Street. Dangerously close, I recall.

"We watched the first plane hit," she tells me.

Winslow was sitting in his window seat facing the World Trade Center—the window seat his father, an artist, had painted with planets, streaking comets, falling stars.

"He said, `I see a plane.' I looked up just in time to see the fireball."

We both glance at Winslow, who's now drawing a large green flower. He's a delicate boy with pale red hair. After the second plane struck, Bryce strapped him into his stroller, then began walking uptown. Striding out of range in case the buildings fell, she didn't look back until they crossed Houston Street.

That day she pushed the stroller all the way to her parents-in-law's apartment on the Upper East Side. And that night, she had an asthma attack, probably brought on by the stress, exertion, and ashy air.

Though she didn't want to get in the way of any rescue efforts, Bryce finally left Winslow with her husband and in-laws and checked herself into St. Luke's.

"Was it hard being in the hospital?" What I think but don't say out loud is that being separated from family in the hours following the attack must have been unbearable.

Gracie lays down her chalk, then runs along the string of alphabet letters painted down the playground's middle. When she reaches the M, I rise to follow her.

"It wasn't hard at all," Bryce shouts after me. "They were so happy to see me, they kept waking me up all night long to offer me sandwiches and stool softeners. You see, they had no one else to help."

God Is Our Shelter (September 27)

The missionaries who sometimes encamp near the southwest entrance to Tompkins Square Park are out in force today.

On folding tables before the wrought-iron fence sit a coffee urn, a caldron of soup, and aluminum trays of cinnamon rolls. Homeless men and a woman or two stand around holding Styrofoam cups and the white-spiraled pastries. They're eating, some of them ravenously, or staring off into space.

A man in grime-stiffened pants takes a couple of steps backward, almost colliding with the stroller. "Excuse me," I say, slowly maneuvering Gracie through the throng.

The missionaries wear Army surplus clothes and have the hard, faded look of survivors, so it's not always easy to tell them from the poor. A smiling man behind the coffee urn offers me a cup of coffee.

"No thank you," I tell him.

Before I can break free, a man wearing green fatigues steps into the stroller's path. He's in his fifties, his buzz cut salted with white frizz. Staring deeply into my eyes, he hands me a pamphlet, then moves out of my way.

As I tuck the pamphlet into the diaper bag, I steal a glance at the color photograph on the cover. Three firemen stand before the skeleton of the World Trade Center. Stripped down to bare gothic spires, the ruins look ageless, beautiful.

That night I study the photo more closely. Two of the men wear gas masks; the third has an oxygen tank strapped to his back. Smoke rising from the muddy ground makes the shattered wall seem farther away than it actually is. Mist or smoke casts a veil over everything. The brightest objects in the frame are the firemen's white and yellow protective-gear stripes, which must have reflected the camera's flash.

Maybe it's the glossy context of the image, on a religious tract safely removed from the news, that lets me actually look at the quiet, horrific, lovely image.

Floating above the wreckage in black letters are the words "God Is Our Shelter and Strength."

NOWHERE THEY'RE NOT (SEPTEMBER 27)

My husband has just returned from his third attempt to visit Ground Zero. This time, he and Breyten managed to get past the Canal Street cordons. Armed with their faculty ID's and a lie about helping students retrieve possessions from a downtown dorm, they came within two blocks of the site.

"I don't know what you think you're doing, but go on ahead," an officer told them.

Chuck is quiet. His eyes are blank. It's as if he has awakened from a long sleep.

What did he see? How was it different from the news?

"I can't say," he tells me.

In the ten years I've known him, he's never been at a loss for words. He loves to, has to, find the right phrase to ensnare the thought of the moment. Listening to him reminds me of our daughter as an infant trying to touch a streak of light. The same fascination, the same joy.

It's been weeks since he's talked like that. The pleasure has leached out of language for me, too. I can't seem to really read or write. Though I've been able to leaf through Kafka's parables and the Bible, newspapers and schoolwork are about all I can manage. Driven to record, I write in my notebook every day, but the sentences have flattened out. The loops and lines occupy two dimensions only. There can be no meanings beyond the words' first meanings, no alternate readings ripening below. I can't bear the thought of creating pregnant language, which seems sacrilegious now. Death on this scale makes art offensive.

That's only partly the reason, though. What was real has been vaporized. I can't trust that things exist, so signifiers standing for ideas of things have become shadows cast by air.

"Are you okay?" I ask.

"I don't know." Chuck sits down on the couch. Gracie, thankfully, is asleep. She's why I haven't joined him and Breyten on their forays ever closer to the destroyed World Trade Center. For her sake, I have to keep myself as unshattered as possible.

I get him a glass of water. He takes it without looking at me.

It's not like him to dramatize his emotions.

"Do you need to lie down?"

"No."

Gently, because I need to know, I ask him again to tell me what he saw.

"The rubble was about a hundred feet high."

This fact tells me nothing. I try to draw the story out of him.

Yes, there was dust. Yes, the smell was awful.

"Everyone was very solemn," he says.

After they left the scene, Chuck walked alone to City Hall Park. He hadn't eaten that day, he says, and felt weak.

"I think I fainted."

"You *think?*"

"I sat on a bench. Time passed. I don't know how much time."

Once more I try to get him to lie down. When he refuses, I go into the kitchen to make him some tea.

That night, after we turn off the news, he says it was because the mound of debris wasn't just debris but the place where thousands of people were buried.

"Not buried in any traditional sense," he says. "They were part of the rubble. The rubble was them."

The blank but still-luminous screen fades to gray.

"And it's not just the rubble," he tells me. "They're in the air all around us. They're everywhere. There's nowhere they're not."

DREAMS (SEPTEMBER 28)

Life seems to be returning to its former shape in that an hour or two can pass without the memory of what happened pulling at me like the web of a new scar.

But tonight I dream of a house in the desert. A strong wind is blowing. Yellow-brown dust as thick as dirt inches under the door. Wind pounds the walls. A rhythm emerges. The wind is someone breathing. It is someone's beating heart.

Then I'm floating alone in a beautiful swimming pool. The water beneath me is as dark as water in a deep ocean. The skin over its surface gleams like cellophane.

The pool, I come to realize, is in a very tall building. The walls of the building are made of glass. A barely seen city lies far below.

Without a sound, the water swells. The smooth lip of a wave curls over the edge. Soon, the pool will overflow.

October, November

Signs of Mourning (October 1)

Outside the firehouse on Great Jones Street is a metal rack filled with bouquets and pots of yellow and rust-colored chrysanthemums. Votive candles burn, their flames almost invisible in the bright afternoon sun.

Memorials like this have collected in front of fire and police stations across the city, whether or not any personnel were lost. But the sheer number of flowers and candles—and the purple bunting that hangs above the arched brick entryway like a dark rainbow—is a clear sign that death came here.

The door to the firehouse is open. Four firefighters stand within the shadows. Three wear protective gear, just the pants and suspenders; they must have returned from a call and are in the process of stripping down. The yellow stripes around their ankles glow. The pants are so huge they could belong to men built on a much larger scale than the actual men inside.

When Chuck and I walk by, I solemnly nod. One of the firemen, meeting my eyes, nods back. He must be used to reverent gestures like this.

The wind catches, lifts the purple cloth. Chuck tells me, "My father used to hang those."

My father-in-law, who died before I could meet him, worked for many years hanging banners and pennants, those small bright triangles that herald the opening of a new supermarket or convenience store.

One day, before we were married, when we were still anxious to find out everything about each other, Chuck pointed at a plaque affixed to a light pole on Sixth Avenue. The plaque said "Bolivia." I stared at it, waiting. He then told me that his father had been hired to put up the plaques with the flags and names of nations when Sixth Avenue was renamed Avenue of the Americas.

"Only no one calls it Avenue of the Americas," he said. "At least no one from New York."

And now, eight years into our marriage, a union sealed by love and loss, my husband, speaking of the mourning drapes we've just seen, says, "If my father was alive today, and if he was still working, he'd be very, very busy."

HOMECOMING (OCTOBER 7)

The squad car's cherry lights slash FDR Drive with faint red streaks. A sign above the barricade says that the Fourteenth

Street exit is blocked to all vehicular traffic. Fourteenth Street, where the Con Ed plant stands like a brick fortress with smokestack turrets, is the exit we usually take when we return from the country.

I glance at Chuck.

"No problem," he says. "We'll go on Houston."

"City!" Gracie yells from her car seat in the back. She loves her city, with its cars, buses, trucks, and tall buildings. So many things to see.

We're coming home from Saugerties after a long weekend upstate, our first time away since September 11. I had wanted to leave soon after, to save Gracie from the smoke, but Chuck insisted on staying. To leave, he said, would be like leaving the side of a wounded relative. I weakly argued, then gave in. The thought of waiting with the baby on checkpoint lines or in lanes crammed with traffic tipped the scale in his favor. Besides, he had a point.

During the three nights in our bungalow, I slept as deeply as the mother of a toddler is able. We didn't read a single paper, didn't turn on the news. In the afternoons I rocked Gracie to sleep in the hammock, staring up at the yellow and green leaves until I too drifted off. Echoing across the mountains in my dreams was the hum of a chainsaw, the tinny tap-tap-tap of gunfire.

On East Fifth Street, Chuck angles past the orange hazard cones that nearly block the crosswalk. All of the parking spots are taken, unusual at this hour on a Sunday morning. Chuck maneuvers in front of a hydrant across the street from our apartment building. We can count on being safe from tickets for an hour or two, enough time to get unloaded and settle Gracie upstairs.

While I'm unbuckling her straps, I hear my husband talking to someone. The driver's-side window fills with the uniformed chest of a police officer.

Shit, I think, *we're going to have to move.*

Getting out of the car, I'm struck by how young the cop is. He's Korean or Chinese, and he's saying we can stay for a while.

"Only, move as soon as possible," he adds. "Two hours ago, we started bombing Afghanistan."

The reason for the blockades around the power and police stations spins into focus. The country is in a state of emergency preparedness, a state of war. The new wave of death has already begun.

I glance at the officer who, I see now, is definitely Chinese. He's in danger. The whole world is in danger.

"Take care of yourself," I tell him.

The urgency in my voice startles me. Ducking back into the car, I touch Gracie's cheek. She has been sitting there without fussing, a small miracle of self-restraint for a kid her age.

"You're my good and patient girl," I murmur.

EXCUSES (OCTOBER 8)

On the way to school, I make the mistake of glancing at the *Times* displayed in a vending machine on Fifth Avenue.

Scrabbling through my purse, I find enough change to buy it. In my office, instead of using the few minutes before class to brush my hair and leaf through the text, I skim the article that caught my eye.

The bombing of Afghanistan is only one aspect of what's being called the war on terror. The Bush administration foresees "overt and covert" action in Malaysia, Indonesia, the Philippines. There seems to be no end to the violence, or to the silence that sanctions it.

"What are your reactions?" I ask my students.

In the semi-darkness they stare up at the image projected onto the screen. It's a news graphic of the Philippines with the southernmost islands highlighted in a color that's supposed to be red but which, cast onto the white surface, looks pink. Columns of text drift below.

"Pretty scary," says Megan.

"Does this mean we're going to have a world war?" William asks.

"What do you think?" I ask. "What *is* 'world war'?"

The class is a writing class. I should now pause to suggest that they free-write, then read their paragraphs out loud, but my cheeks are still hot with the shock of discovery. Blankly, I listen to my students discuss the news. I'm tired of pretending to teach. Whatever made me think I was capable of teaching during a moment in history too big to even begin to absorb?

After class is over and the others have left the room,

Ragoso, whom I like very much, apologizes for not having written the paper due that day.

"It's been a little crazy." He smiles, then tilts the bill of his Mets cap up to reveal expressive brown eyes. Ragoso is Muslim, from Indonesia, one of the targeted countries. During the class discussion, he had not uttered a single word.

Now he tells me that his father, traveling out of the country on business, was detained and unable for four days to call anyone with the news he was alive and well. Also, he says, his mother's attempts to flee Indonesia were thwarted when the American embassy there closed.

"So I went to Boston, where my sister is. We spent the weekend waiting by the phone."

His eyes gleam. I can't tell if he's crying.

"How are things now?"

Ragoso tilts his cap back down, hiding his face. "My mom's still in Jakarta."

While I consider whether or not to hug him, he takes a half step back and once more meets my eyes.

"It won't happen again," he says.

I'm momentarily confused. Is Ragoso predicting the future? Does he know something most North Americans don't? While U.S. reporters were researching and writing the coy stories that make up today's headlines, Ragoso's family had been swept into the storm of the semi-secret worldwide war already under way.

"I'll get that paper to you on Wednesday," he says. "I mean, if you're willing to accept it."

He *is* crying. A tear drips down the side of his nose.

"That's okay," I tell him. "Take as much time as you need."

MORAL COURAGE (OCTOBER 10)

The body artist guides the tube of brown paste over my hand. Soon scales and florets appear on my skin.

"You're good," I tell her. "Have you been doing this long?"

She sets down the tube, tucks a strand of blonde hair behind her ear. "Almost nine years."

The wet henna glistens like chocolate. When it dries, it will stain me with the designs I've seen on my East Indian students after family weddings. I'm not going to a wedding, though. I have stopped into an open workshop at the art and design school where I teach to get my hand painted. A gentle distraction from war and death is just what I need.

I'm very tired. I'm tired of being tired, of going to bed exhausted, then startling awake at three in the morning. I'm tired of walking into class having forgotten to bring the day's handouts, my folders, the text. I'm tired of forgetting just about everything. I can't seem to hold on to thoughts or ideas; the threads snap clean before they can form. Most of all, I'm tired of being unable to really write, or feel language pearl up inside.

The design is finished. It's tear shaped.

"What does it mean?"

I want the swirl on my hand to stand for life or wisdom or

love. At the risk of committing cultural appropriation, I want to be touched by a tradition that might console me.

"Nothing, really," the body artist says. "I found it while researching rug designs in Madras. It's a pattern you can see in many weavings from the region."

She daubs the drying henna with a cotton ball soaked in sugared lemon water. Giving me a candle, she instructs me to hold the flame close. The warmth, she says, will result in a richer dye.

The studio fills with the scent of melting wax. All around me, students are quietly painting henna onto their own hands. This has proved to be pretty much the peaceful moment I'd hoped for. When I offer my thanks and leave for home, I carry the memory of that peace with me.

By the next morning, the paste has flaked off. As directed, I rub the skin with olive oil. The design deepens to a dark reddish brown. It's a part of me yet not me. Throughout the teaching day, I glance down at the intricate lines. They're a reminder that this depression must end.

But that night, on the walk home, I realize that with my *hapa* woman's dark hair, skin, and eyes, and now with my hennaed hand, I might be seen as South Asian instead of half Chinese. I might be seen as the Enemy Other, whatever that means.

Pulling down my sleeve, I hide the design.

The next moment, I cringe at my smallness, my willingness to separate myself from people who are in danger because of ethnicity or nation. I'm no better—I'm probably worse—than the Chinese Americans who wore "I am Chinese" buttons after World War II to escape violence aimed at Japanese.

Wincing at my lack of moral courage, I push the sleeve back up.

Dreams (October 11)

I am walking through a silent department store. The shelves are bare of merchandise. The space is too vast and dimly lit to see the end of. No other customers are in sight.

I am sitting in a room hot with the glare of umbrellaed lights. Video cameras point at the empty podium. Still cameras click, then whir as the film rewinds.

Because I hold a steno pad in one hand, I must be a journalist, a job I held in waking life for twelve years. Looking down, I notice that I'm wearing a *cheongsam*, the red silk embroidered with golden thread. It's a Chinese wedding dress.

The fact of my clothing terrifies me. If they realize I'm Asian, they'll kill me.

Wandering through the apartment we've lived in for years, I come to my husband's office. His desk has been swept clean. Papers lie scattered on the floor. The nakedness of his desktop tells me our home has been abandoned. I have nowhere to go.

THE NEWS ABOUT K. (OCTOBER 15)

Tom pushes the door open wider so I can enter his office.

He's the director of freshman English. At midnight last Thursday, a first-year student named K. jumped off the roof of the Twelfth Street dormitory. I'm meeting with Tom to get some guidance about how to handle her suicide. Though K. wasn't my student, my freshmen knew her. Almost all of them live in the same dorm.

Giving Tom a hug, I say, "I'm sorry."

K. was in his class. I can't imagine what it will be like for him to walk into the room and feel it swell with her absence.

He smiles sadly. His door clicks shut.

"How well did you get to know her?"

How well have any of us gotten to know our kids in this disordered time? There was no note, he says, no prior warning. No one could have predicted it.

"The aftermath was ugly," he says.

Most of the dorm residents saw K.'s body lying in the courtyard. For the duration of the police investigation, which lasted several hours, no one was permitted to leave the building.

"I also should tell you that a number of your students saw her fall."

Hands lying inert on the armrests, Tom leans back in his chair. He has finished the grim recitation.

The blurred bodies of the World Trade Center jumpers

hang before the bright glass. Given the choice between fire and void, they chose the void. What pain K. must have felt to have elected to die this way. Was she aware of how her death's image would become one with the pictures of those other deaths?

"Did September 11—?"

Uncharacteristically, Tom cuts me off. "No," he says. "Suicide is the end of a gradual process. This was coming for years."

He rises, and I do, too. It's time for us to teach.

COPING (OCTOBER 15)

No one is absent, I'm surprised to see. Without having been asked to do so, they've already pulled their chairs in a circle.

Looking into their eyes, I wish I had something helpful to say. Instead I tell them how sorry I am. Then I listen to my voice repeat what Tom told me, that while the police investigation isn't yet closed, the circumstances of K.'s death do indeed point to suicide.

Never before have I been so aware of the act of standing in front of a class. How inadequate my body is. My mouth forms words, most of them meaningless. What if one of the children sitting here now is nursing thoughts of suicide? What are the signs? I scan their solemn faces.

"Does anyone want to talk?"

Expecting silence, I'm slightly shocked to see the hands shoot up.

"I know this sounds bad," Megan says, "but I'm really mad at her. She did it without any consideration for the people around her."

Stunned, I nod. "Does anyone share Megan's feelings?"

Heads bob. One by one, they air their fury. If K. was so miserable, why didn't she tell any of her friends? Why did she do it? Why did she have to do it where everyone could see?

My own anger rises. A young woman is dead, I think. Don't any of you mourn?

The assignment now, I tell them, is to write a letter about their reactions.

"Can I write to myself?" asks Selena. "I don't want anyone to see it."

"Then no one has to."

While they bend over their notebooks or tap laptop keys, I consider my own flash of rage, which I hope none of them saw. I wasn't in the dormitory that awful night; I have no right to judge. Maybe their anger is useful, protective armor against the shock. It seems to indicate that they haven't fully registered the fact of K.'s death. To voice anger suggests that, deep down, they believe K. might be able to respond.

Glancing at my watch, I see that almost fifteen minutes remain till class is over. Rising from the circle of chairs, I settle behind the desk and wait for them to finish.

DIRECT ADDRESS (OCTOBER 16)

Most of the letters are to no one.

Some are written to the writers' friends. Ragoso addresses his to K. herself. He understands how she felt, so lonely, so far from home.

"You write beautifully about difficult feelings," I scrawl on the back of the page. "Please see me after class; I want to know how you're doing."

Finished with the handwritten letters, I turn on my computer to retrieve the electronic offerings. The letter from William that flashes across the screen is addressed directly to me. Hitting the scroll key, I'm perturbed by how easily he ripped through the distance I'd tried to impose between us. Normally I'd be pleased by his metafictional insight and courage, but today I feel too vulnerable to offer praise.

William usually is a reluctant writer who doesn't do more than what's required. For this assignment, though, he's summoned easily a thousand words.

"I'm not sure what I think about doing this," he begins, "but I might as well get a few things off my chest."

He has titled the letter, the essay, "October 11." Counting the days backward on my fingers, I confirm that October 11 was indeed the day K. chose to die. What follows is a meticulous account of the hours that began with K.'s death and stretched into dawn.

William and two of K.'s roommates were studying in K.'s

suite when they saw something large flash past the window. The bed he stood on to see what had fallen was K.'s, he wrote, "only I didn't know how ironic that was."

Looking down, he saw a dark blob lying in the courtyard. While he watched, the blob grew darker, the darkness spreading around it. After a while a police officer knocked on their door. When one of the women went to answer it, the officer ran into the bathroom. "We could hear him throwing up."

That night no one slept. The next day, William dozed for a couple of hours on the couch of a suite safely facing the street. Since returning to his own suite on the courtyard side, he's had trouble sleeping.

As I read, I can't help thinking that this is the best writing of William's I've seen. Urgent. Expressive. Exact. He's still writing only what's absolutely necessary, but death has enlarged the field, given him eloquence and authority.

It has made the work real.

THERAPY (OCTOBER 19)

The dimmer switch allows Mary's patients to make the room as bright or dark as they need it to be.

I prefer deep dusk. It's been three years since my last visit. Three years ago, from late winter through the end of spring, I went to Mary twice a week for what our insurance company called "bereavement counseling."

The first time I saw her, Chuck and I went together.

Early on in the session, he pushed the tissue box near us out of reach.

"It looks like a karyotype," he said.

Before Mary slid the box out of sight behind her, I saw that the fuzzy X's floating over the cardboard surface did resemble the photo image of our first baby's flawed chromosomes. With a felt-tipped pen the genetic counselor had slowly circled three stubby X's—three where in a normal fetus there would be only two. Later I would realize that he must have to do this every time, to show people a truth they couldn't bear to believe.

I am here to see Mary today because K.'s suicide, on top of everything else, is more than I can handle. I don't feel strong enough to teach, to help my students through this. The paralysis doesn't end when I leave the classroom. Unlike William, I haven't been able to get things off my chest. Writing in my journal hasn't helped. I can't possess the words, feel them, make them mine. They blurt out all over the page, as graceless as biology gone wrong. I haven't found a way to tell the story, a strategy which in the past has helped me carve a path away from sorrow. At this point, I'm not even sure what the story is.

After softly knocking, Mary opens the door. We hug hello, then I hand her a picture of my daughter, who's seated in her high chair with an upside-down cereal bowl on her head. We talk for a few moments about how wonderful Gracie is before getting down to business.

Soon I realize that I'm slightly embarrassed to be here. How self-indulgent of me to mourn. I suspect I'm wasting Mary's time. Others must be more in need of her tender services.

But she carefully listens, then dispenses advice that goes deeper than the words, her attention itself a kind of balm.

"You know," she adds, "after the attack, a group of us met to discuss how to help other people when we ourselves felt so shattered."

These were extraordinary times—the first time, in this city at least, that so many were plagued by the same grief. No one really knew how to proceed. The group of therapists decided that all they could do was the best they could manage.

Smiling, she rises from her chair. Following her cue I get up off the sofa. My hour is over.

CONQUEROR OF THE WORLD (OCTOBER 20)

In the shadows of a construction scaffolding on First Avenue, Chuck and I run into Jahangir and his parents.

Jahangir is a few months younger than Gracie, but he's a big boy, already taller and heavier than she is. He's wearing jeans, a denim shirt, and a small blue fishing hat. Gripping his mother's hand, he stares at Gracie in her stroller.

"His name mean 'conqueror of the world,'" Jahangir's father said last spring, when we introduced ourselves to each other in the playground.

What I remember most about that lost time is the wild joy of children released from winter. Bright green flowers fell from the elms, onto the blacktop and slides. Even before I learned the meaning of his son's name, Jahangir's father made me feel slightly uneasy because of his loud cheerfulness and way of standing a few inches too close when talking.

"What a beautiful girl!" he shouted the first time he saw Gracie.

Leaning down, he rubbed her head and pinched her cheeks. Two or three of his top teeth were missing. The surrounding teeth were mottled with decay.

His wife barely spoke to us, possibly because of her English. I've never seen either of them wear anything but traditional clothing, he in his white skullcap and flowing trousers, she in her dark dresses and head scarves.

"How are you today, beauty?" Jahangir's father now yells. "Look at how big she's getting!"

He brushes his knuckles against Gracie's cheek.

Chuck asks after Jahangir, who, we learn, is recovering from the measles. Faint red circles like small bruises pock his face.

"Poor boy," I murmur.

"He's getting better." Jahangir's father grins. It's then I see that his mouth is filled with new teeth as white as a clean page.

After we say good-bye, then walk another block closer to home, Chuck says, "You're thinking what I'm thinking."

I am and hate that I am, hate the fear that gilds my vision and inspires feelings I've warned my students about succumbing to.

Nodding, I take a damp wipe out of the diaper bag and dab our daughter's face where Jahangir's father touched it.

DREAMS (OCTOBER 24)

I am living alone in the penthouse apartment of a skyscraper. The shelves are filled with books, the floor covered by a dark red Persian rug. An elaborately carved door leads out on to the terrace.

Suddenly, the apartment is packed with people. A party of some kind is under way. One man wants us to attach bombs to our bodies. The bombs are contained in black bands that look like fanny packs. By his gestures—he doesn't appear to speak English—I understand that he wants me to strap a bomb around my forehead.

The partygoers, all wearing their bombs, have been transformed into my students. The man who brought us the explosives is gone. In the moment before our deaths, we are safe.

I say to them, "Shall we follow the lesson plan or write letters to people we love? I myself want to write letters."

IRONY (OCTOBER 31)

A name is now attached to the sixty-one-year-old New York woman who died of inhalation anthrax earlier this week. She is Kathy T. Nguyen, a Vietnamese immigrant who worked in the stockroom of the Manhattan Eye, Ear, and Throat Hospital.

Kathy Nguyen led what the *Times* calls a "simple" and "discreet" life—so discreet that investigators are having trouble piecing together her final days. Apparently, there are no friends or family to question.

Famous only in death, Nguyen is the fourth American living on the Eastern Seaboard to succumb to the disease. I know that her death and the other deaths are supposed to make me feel afraid, but I'm not. My lack of fear can't be called courage; it has more to do with emotional overload.

"Can you imagine?" Chuck says. "She survived the war and came here, only to die like this."

The irony cuts too deeply for me to think about the lonely death of Kathy Nguyen for long. "Kathy" would be the name she took on like armor when she came to this country, a name the strangers around her would be able to pronounce.

I wonder if her real name will ever be known.

PERMISSION (NOVEMBER 8)

While Dublin and Gracie bang on the piano, Adeola plays with a silver egg and Jack pinches Play-Doh into tiny primary-colored balls.

In this quiet moment—none of the children are crying or bent on undue destruction—the mothers talk about Sharon and Jon's decision to move back to Wisconsin. They had planned to move in May but, given the circumstances, are thinking of leaving next month.

"If you were me, what would you do?" Sharon asks.

Liselot says, "Since you're going anyway, it would be better to go now."

Driving Liselot's remark is the calculus haunting us all: Leaving New York might equal our children's survival.

"There's no reason to feel guilty, if that's what you're thinking."

"But I do."

Though I've lived most of my adult life in New Mexico and the Midwest, I grew up in New York and its suburbs. I consider myself a New Yorker. I haven't seriously considered abandoning the city where Chuck and I and now our daughter were born. Right after September 11, yes, I had wanted to flee. But flight was linked to the idea of return. New York will always be the place I come back to. It's home.

My love for the city is tinged with hubris. Like most New Yorkers, I like to feel that I am tougher than those who can't cut it here.

"I understand," I say.

My friend Sharon, who doesn't have deep roots in this town, is asking for permission to leave.

"If I were you," I tell her, "I'd definitely leave now."

AN ORDINARY DISASTER (NOVEMBER 12)

The woman behind the counter tucks my liter bottle of water into a plastic bag, then says, "Did you hear about the plane? Terrible news."

What news?

The crash occurred less than an hour ago, so the details being reported are few. Several minutes after taking off from JFK, a passenger plane fell out of the sky, plowing into a residential neighborhood in Queens.

"Queens? Where in Queens?"

"Far Rockaway, I think."

I thank her, then walk quickly to my office. Tossing my backpack on the floor, I tap my grandmother and Aunt Mui's number into the phone. Far Rockaway is where my Great-aunt Faith lives, a few blocks from the beach.

Mui tells me that she's already gotten through to Faith, who's fine. Her house is across the causeway from the crash site. Though plane parts and debris—and human remains, too, though Mui tactfully omits mentioning them—lie strewn over the neighborhood, nothing seems to have landed on Faith's property.

Now that I know my family is safe, I can ask the next question.

"Do they think it's terrorism?"

"No," says Mui. "According to the news, there's no evidence of terrorism." At least, she adds, none of the witnesses who watched the plane go down heard or saw an explosion.

"Any idea how many were on board?"

"They're saying two hundred fifty."

"What about on the ground?"

"A few. They don't know for sure."

The tension that's kept my breathing shallow since I heard about the crash releases its grip on my rib cage. It's probably not terrorism. And the number of dead, only two hundred fifty, seems insignificant.

A second later, I'm dismayed by my own reaction. How awful to feel relief over a disaster that a few months ago would have sent the city into shock.

What have we become that death on this scale is ordinary?

WINTER

THE MEANING OF DEATH (DECEMBER 20)

In the middle of lunch—steamed carrots and rice fried with the leftover broccoli—Gracie stops eating to stare at me.

"Mommy, don't die," she says.

Though she has spoken very clearly, I can't believe what I've just heard.

"What did you say, honey?"

"Mommy, don't die."

In the light arrowing through the kitchen windows, her hazel eyes look more blue than green. She doesn't seem anxious or afraid, just determined to be heard.

"What does 'die' mean?" I ask.

Without pausing, she says, "Sophie died."

Sophie, her godmother Joan's dog, suddenly sickened and died earlier this month. Death, I told my daughter, doubting the wisdom of my definition, is when animals or people go away and never come back.

Cupping her soy-sauce-smeared cheeks, I look deeply into her eyes, the way I do whenever I'm trying to impart a vital lesson. With a conviction I can't feel, I tell her, "Don't worry, darling, Mommy's not going to die. I'm not going to die for a long, long time."

THE SIMPLEST POSSIBLE LANGUAGE (DECEMBER 20)

A musty odor taints the air. The room they've put me in is crowded with garbage bags stuffed with old coats. The brown arm of a leather jacket protrudes from one open plastic mouth.

"Holiday clothing drive." There's a hint of apology in Officer Genovese's voice. Like the other policemen involved in the case, Officer Genovese is brisk but unfailingly polite. This politeness, added to the fact of how quickly the two squad cars pulled up to the corner, within a minute after I called 911, has dulled fear's edge. At least I've stopped trembling.

In the large room just beyond stands the man who took my purse. He is, as I told the 911 operator, a black man in his thirties wearing a black jacket and a black cap.

The jacket is slipping off his shoulders, but because of the handcuffs he can't pull it back on. He's staring at me. His expression is blank, as if he's never seen me before.

When it happened I was sitting in a café on Avenue A. For the first time since September 11, I was writing a story, wrapped in a net of dreams, and didn't notice when the purse stupidly slung over the back of my chair disappeared.

The purse is a leopard-print number just large enough to hold my wallet and keys. I bought it at Kmart for $4.99. Proud of my ingenuity—who would think to look in Kmart for stylish accessories?—I tell anyone who asks where I got it and for how much.

A man at the table next to mine said something to alert me. We both watched the other man walk out of the café with my purse. He and I followed. The three of us stood on the corner. The day was very cold.

"This belongs to Betty," said the man with my purse.

"No, it belongs to this woman. Why don't you give it back?"

"It's Betty's.

"No, hers."

No voices were raised. We might have been talking about the weather, or the day's news. Without another word, the man handed me the bag. When three other men rushed out of the café, shouting, he just stood there, as if the commotion didn't involve him.

Near the desk where he now waits to be booked is a Christmas tree hung with paper angels. The angels wear blue construction-paper uniforms with double rows of crayoned yellow buttons. Instead of a star on top of the tree, there's an American flag.

I realize that I might have been hurt or killed, but that's not what's bothering me. What's bothering me is the understanding that the whole sequence of events went by without leaving a clear imprint on memory. When Officer Genovese questioned me, I was almost unable to respond. What had I seen? When did I know that the purse the man held was mine? What did he even look like? I stare at the cuffed hands, which seem detached from the rest of his body. If I really interrogate myself, all I find are a jumble of still frames that make no intrinsic sense. A black-spotted purse. The gray sky. A glass door swinging shut. Can I claim to remember anything?

Now Officer Genovese leans into the coat-filled room where I sit.

"Here, ma'am."

He gives me my bag. In his other hand are three sheets of paper, murky Xeroxes of the cheap purse and credit cards within. Evidence.

The suspect has priors, he's saying. The DA's office will get in touch with me. The grand jury won't take much of my time, a half an hour at the most.

"All you'll have to do is describe what happened using the simplest possible language. 'Yes, he took my purse. No, he didn't have permission to possess it.'"

Officer Genovese glances up at the clock on the wall. It's then I notice that it tells military time, each station of the hour cleanly divided into black and white halves. Like the night and day they symbolize.

"That's all?"

"Yes, ma'am," he says. "That's all."

Testimony (December 28)

I haven't been to Ground Zero till now because I wasn't sure I could take it. But today I have to go downtown anyway, to testify against the man who stole my purse.

Hanging in the grand jury waiting room is a Vermeer print, the woman and two men within the frame washed in the painter's honey light. Officer Genovese and Greg, the men who got my purse back, sit with me in the rows of long, pew-like seats.

To make small talk, I ask Officer Genovese about September 11.

No, he didn't rush down to the disaster site. Off duty at the time, he was called in to help man the Fourteenth Street blockades.

"I think I must've gained twenty pounds since then." Grinning, he pats his flat stomach. "All the restaurant owners kept bringing over food. Out of consideration I tried to taste everything, but you just can't eat it all."

He leans back against the wall. A moment later, his eyes close.

It's almost noon before our case is called. Officer Genovese and Greg testify first. Within a few minutes, the assistant district attorney waves me into the courtroom.

Standing in the witness box, I raise my right hand, then swear to tell the truth. Prompted by the assistant district attorney, I recite the narrative of the theft. While I speak, some of the jurors seated in the amphitheater above don't even

glance down at me. My voice drones on. Most of the questions are framed so that my answers must take the form of
monosyllables. Yes. No. Yes.

"Are there any questions?" the ADA asks the jury.

No. I am excused.

A moment later, the ADA returns to the waiting room. The
grand jury indicted the defendant on sixteen felony counts, he
says. Smiling, he adds, "Justice was served." Now if Greg and I
will come down to the office with him and fill out our witness forms, we will receive ten dollars apiece. "Allegedly it
covers the cost of carfare and lunch. Compliments of the State
of New York."

Outside, it's freezing. Stopping at a pushcart, I buy a bottle
of water and a knish. The relief at having performed my part
without stumbling has given way to a sense of uneasiness. Justice was served, but what does that mean?

Eight of the felony counts against my purse snatcher
correspond to the eight credit cards I carry, not because I
use them all but because we keep acquiring new cards in
order to endlessly shuffle off debt without racking up
interest. Does justice consist of a family spending beyond
its means and a woman's unkempt wallet? Does it come
from Greg's alertness and bravery, from the civic courage
fanned by 9/11 that may have prompted the three other
men to rush out of the café and surround the thief before
he could quietly slip away? Does it arise from the fact that
no grand jury would doubt the testimony of an Asian

American woman, a white man, and a police officer against a black man? Besides, who was Betty? The guy said the purse belonged to Betty. If he wasn't acting, maybe he really was insane.

Centre Street flows into Broadway. People crowd the sidewalks, their brightly colored parkas and the way they pause to gaze up at the buildings exposing most of them as out-of-state tourists. And I can't help wondering what would have happened if I'd chosen to not testify. Now that my role in the case is over, I see that I could have demurred at any point along the way. But I was swept up in the flow of events. I went along. I followed the law. I cooperated. I did my duty as a citizen. I obeyed, didn't raise my voice, didn't have a voice to raise unless you could count Yes and No and Yes.

It's not that I'm ungrateful to Greg and the café Samaritans, or to the cops and legal system that protects people like me. Nor am I unduly sorry that the defendant, who lives in my neighborhood and who, the ADA hinted, has a history of violence, will be spending time in prison. I just wish I knew what the word "justice" means.

The crowd thickens till all I can do is shuffle along. Children waving small American flags ride their parents' shoulders. A man takes slow, panning video footage of the small church stranded among skyscrapers and the thickets of flowers, candles, and fliers left on its iron fence.

Turning west on to Fulton, we pass a pizza parlor, its open

door releasing a rich whiff of tomato sauce and oil. Midway down the block, a row of police sawhorses divides the street. At the bottom is a plywood wall. Beyond the wall gapes empty space. Two tall yellow cranes rise out of the void. Closer to earth, backhoes scoop and disgorge loads of rubble.

This, then, is Ground Zero. Though I'm standing on the brink of the real thing, the Ground Zero of my imagination—the smoking pyre, the air bitter with death, the ashes of the victims mingled with the ashes of their attackers—is actually more real to me.

I'm still thinking of the indicted man, who even now is being led away to whatever jail they'll keep him in till his case is pleaded or heard. "With all his priors," Officer Genovese said, "you won't have to worry about seeing the defendant again for a long, long time."

The truth is, whatever injury I suffered at his hands—the minute or two I was separated from my purse, the inconvenience, the fear—is nothing compared to what he'll endure in retribution. And because I'm here at the spectacle of Ground Zero, I can't help thinking of the violence named Justice that has and will be wrought upon the world, with the consent and consenting silence of the American people. With my silence, which I long to break.

The crowd at the sawhorses stands three or four deep. I edge closer.

"There used to be two tall buildings. Remember from the news?" a man is saying.

"What happened to them?"

I can't tell without looking if the child is a girl or boy.

"Don't you remember?" the father is saying. "Some bad men stole our planes and flew them into the buildings. The buildings burned, then fell down."

"Why are we here?"

Surreptitiously, I glance to my left. The child is wearing a cobalt-blue ski jacket and yellow earmuffs. He's about six or seven years old.

"They're not just buildings, they're tombs," says the father, his voice swelling with the awareness that more people than just his son are listening. "We're here to see them so you can tell your children and grandchildren."

And when the boy gives him a sidelong look of bafflement, the precursor of fear, the man adds, "So you can remember for the rest of your life."

Remembering (December 30)

Making a quesadilla for my daughter's lunch, I accidentally leave the Ziploc bag with the cheese too close to the frying pan.

When the plastic touches hot iron, it melts. The chemical odor released is the same one that hung in the air for weeks while the wreckage of the World Trade Center burned.

Tears fill my eyes. I inhale. Deeply.

NEW YEAR'S EVE (DECEMBER 31)

I wake up about ten minutes before the ball is due to drop on Times Square.

The camera is aimed at the crowd. Lifting my head from Chuck's blue-jeaned knees, I notice that the revelers are standing in pens formed by metal gates.

This containment is something new.

"For security, they say," Chuck tells me.

Many of the penned-in people waiting for the year to turn wear fake glasses with sequined frames shaped into the number 2002. Watching their eyes blink and stare through the double zeros, I realize for the first time that the year, like 1991, is a numerical palindrome.

There doesn't seem to be much else to think about the whole business—other than the fact that in a few minutes 2001, the first year of the new millennium, will be left blessedly in the past.

HOLIDAYS (JANUARY 3)

Three rolls' worth of color photos lie spread across the coffee table.

I've spent the last half hour trying to decipher them.

The shots of Gracie and Elena holding long, thin balloons twisted into the shapes of dachshunds must be from Ruby's Hanukkah party. Gracie in her snowflake pajamas pounding on a wooden drum is evidence of Christmas morning. My mother-in-law, Ann, smiling tiredly while winter dusk darkens the window at her back, is Christmas dinner. Christmas Day is my grandmother looking small and disheveled in her thronelike teak chair.

I fan through the pictures again. Vague sensations of pleasure and dread radiate like broken halos around the images of family and friends. The photos attest to days spent rushing from house to house, taking and bearing away bags full of gifts and food.

Despite the evidence before me, though, I'm unable to summon a single concrete memory.

PRETTY FIREBALL (JANUARY 11)

"You know," my mother says, "the most vivid memory I have of nine-eleven is what you told Gracie that day."

"What did I tell her?"

Fast-forwarding the video past the opening credits, I slow to "play" at the start of the first episode. Ever since Humera's visit soon after the buildings fell, *Dreams* has been the baby's favorite film. Showing it guarantees she'll be quiet for the duration of my mother's call.

"You were on the phone with me when the towers collapsed. You began to cry—to wail."

Incandescent mist rises from the forest floor. Hearing my mother say this makes the moment real again. Blurred bodies fall. Smoke in the shape of a building fills the screen. Cumulus clouds tumble down Broadway.

"Then Gracie started to cry, too," my mother continues. "You stopped and said to her, 'Look at the pretty fireball.'"

"I said that?"

"You did."

"I don't remember."

I don't. No memory of having spoken the words exists. Hearing them from my mother, I hear them for the first time. That anyone could have pronounced them at that moment in history astonishes me.

"Oh, look!" Gracie says.

Though she has seen the movie dozens of times before, her voice is bright with wonder.

"Look at what, honey?" my mother says into the receiver, as if her granddaughter could hear.

The boy in the blue kimono springs out from behind the bole of a huge tree. He has been seen, flushed from his hiding place by suspicious fox spirits. The protective mist that's surrounded him till now has disappeared.

"Saw him!" Gracie yells.

"What?" my mother asks.

"*Dreams,* Mom," I tell her. "She's watching Kurosawa's *Dreams.*"

MUSIC (JANUARY 18)

Jessica smiles, then says, "For the next song we'll sing the words 'ice cream' instead of 'mommies' and 'daddies.' Some of our families lost parents on September 11."

Today is the second day that the music class has met. Seated on mats in a circle are about a dozen mothers and nannies holding toddlers or babies on their laps. The music school runs a number of classes for young kids. I wonder if any of the children here belong to the bereaved families, then think, no, Jessica wouldn't have explained the situation so frankly in front of them.

Still, the families would live in the neighborhood. They would go to the same playgrounds, libraries, and bookstores that we do. It would only be a matter of time before Gracie and her sitters or I encounter kids who lost fathers or mothers or both in the attack on the World Trade Center.

Perhaps Gracie already plays with the orphaned children.

I close my eyes. When I open them again, Jessica is swaying from side to side. Taking her lead, the women seated in the circle mimic her slow, stationary dance. To the gentle beat of a lullaby we sing

> May there always be sunshine
> May there always be blue skies
> May there always be ice cream
> May there always be me.

A KIND OF LIE (JANUARY 19)

"Guess who's calling? Jack's mommy!"

Gracie grabs the receiver. Grinning, she nods yes to the

questions Sharon must be posing on the other end. Taking back the phone, I hear someone loudly, wetly breathing.

"Hello, sweet boy," I say. "Can you get your mom?"

I hungrily ask Sharon for news. How is Jack adjusting to his new home? Has John found a job? Are they happy in Milwaukee? Was leaving the right decision?

When it's Sharon's turn to ask the questions, she says, "How is New York?"

I find myself taken aback, on the defensive, as if protecting my wounded city from an outsider's cool gaze.

"Fine," I tell her. "The burned smell's gone. Ever since New Year's it's as if a pall has lifted."

Though the words are true enough, I've just told a kind of lie. I've misrepresented the first collective sigh of relief as a return to normalcy.

By way of correction I add, "Things are getting better, but it's still pretty hard."

I'm grateful when, a moment later, we move on to a new topic.

HEROES (JANUARY 19)

A small film crew has gathered in front of the police station.

At first, I think they're shooting a movie or an episode of *NYPD Blue*, but there are too few cameramen and technicians, four—no, five—of them. They might be NYU film students, but then I remember that it's winter break and school isn't in session. Besides, the men assembled around the tripod are too old to be students, too focused on their task.

The scene they are filming is of a sole officer standing near the tall double doors that enclose the dead-end alley next to the station house. The alley is cobbled with gray paving stones, the same ones that used to cover the streets. In the early 1900's, the alley housed the precinct's horses. Now it's used to store bag upon black plastic bag of garbage.

Within a month after 9/11, a local graffiti artist spray-painted a simple mural on the door to nowhere. A tremendous American flag ripples in an unseen wind. In neon-bright letters against a green background are the words

> To the Community
> With Thanks
> From the 9th Precinct

The officer turns slightly away from the camera's lens so that his face will appear in profile against the painted flag. In his dress uniform, he looks like a cop out of the 1950's. His hands hang palms to the back, causing his torso to take on the rigid posture of a soldier at attention. It's a windless, overcast day, heavy with the chill of snow.

The resolute expression dissolves when he sees me.

"Hi there," he says.

It's Officer Genovese, who arrested my purse snatcher.

"How's it going?" I say. "What's this for?"

A crouching cameraman glances up at me. His dark blue jacket has an NBC logo with interlocking colored rings on the back.

"The Winter Olympics," he says.

I can see it. Officer Genovese's young face against the flag will be part of a montage of New York heroes—the firefighters, police, EMT's, and construction workers at Ground Zero—that will flash across millions of screens for the minute or two before a commercial break.

I nod, then begin to walk away.

Remembering that I haven't said good-bye to Officer Genovese, I spin back around.

"He's a good cop!" I call to the cameramen.

The moment the words leave my mouth, I feel like a liar. I am a liar. It's not that Officer Genovese isn't a good cop. He handled my admittedly uncomplicated case like a pro, but as grateful as I am, I otherwise don't know enough to judge. Caught in the swell of the moment, I have become part of the dangerous sentimental pageant. "Good cop," after all, is one of those empty phrases that masquerade as meaningful, not unlike "the war on terror."

Officer Genovese grins. "Yeah, I took care of you, didn't I?"

Though the double-entendre startles me, I smile. But he has already resumed staring straight ahead at First Avenue, with the quiet expression of a man looking out at the sea.

DREAMS (JANUARY 20)

Though the two skyscrapers resemble the World Trade towers, they're taller and more spectral. Surrounded by the same atmospheric haze that veils mountains, they climb thousands of feet into the air.

When I look again, both buildings are wreathed in black smoke.

I know I should turn on the news. But if I turn on the news I'll have to keep the TV on all the time, and I'm still so tired from the last disaster.

PROFILES IN GRIEF (JANUARY 21)

I wake up at 3 A.M. thinking of the *Times* articles about those who died in the World Trade Center attack.

When the pieces first started to appear, I anxiously scanned the names and faces for someone I might have known, someone from deep in the past, since everyone in my immediate circle was accounted for. Drawn to the pages by sorrow and dread, I carefully read each one.

As the weeks wore on, I continued to read out of respect. These days I skim whenever I have the time, casually searching for people who interest me, people I might have wanted to meet.

My years as a journalist return. Each brief, accompanied by a head shot, measures five column inches. Each lists the subject's hobbies, quirks, and pleasures, the kinds of details that almost never make it into a real obit.

She doted on her daughter.

Everything was about his boys.

Her life was bracketed by historic events.

He prided himself on his world-class cooking.

For as long as anyone can remember, he wanted to be a New York City fireman.

An obituary usually flattens a life into a collection of facts. The facts become points to connect, like stars in a constellation. Span the light years between and you'll see archers and goddesses gleaming in the night sky. Distance allows obit readers to view the dead person whole. Only then can we begin the work of mourning.

The *Times* articles, though, come closer to profiles, which are written about the living. They're even collectively titled "Profiles in Grief." Reading them, it's as if the people they're about aren't really dead.

It might have been this thought, spun into the fabric of a forgotten dream, that startled me out of sleep.

UNTITLED (JANUARY 21)

I begin writing a book about 9/11.

Before now, each passage I've written on the subject has had its separate life. Like most journals, mine has no sense of continuity. Every day stands alone. The pages from those days are patches of color, flashes that exist only while I write them. Leafing through my notebooks, I read whole paragraphs I don't recall having written. They're as lost to memory as experience itself.

Rediscovery is an aspect of reading journals, but I've forgotten so much about September 11 and the days that followed, forgetfulness an unconscious trick to stem the pain, I'm surprised by what I read. Did I really live through this?

Here's the story, I think. It's a story about remembering.

After the first wave of pleasure recedes, though, I start to worry. I don't feel any less passion for the project—my sense of clarity is so sharp it unnerves me—but I'm reluctant to lose any remaining sensations of a practically holy time. The visions from September 11 live inside me but sometimes beyond my reach. Busy days at school and home have already done their damage. I've been writing long enough to know that deliberately describing my sense memories will finish the job of killing them off. If I expose them to air, they'll be gone, transmuted by language into shells given shape by what's no longer alive.

On the other hand, I have to write. I have to *get* it right. I'll call the book *In the Life After* because the life before is already gone.

GRAFFITI (JANUARY 23)

The toilet stall closest to the window—the one that, without thinking, I usually select—has been coated with fresh paint.

This fact surprises me. New paint is a rarity at my college in the best of times, and now there's a spending freeze in place due to the recession and loss of tuition from students who, because of fear or 9/11 deaths in the family, have withdrawn from school.

Then I notice that only one wall has been repainted. A few words bleed through the whiteness.

FUCK YOU
YOU HAVE NO RIGHT
TO BE HERE

Beneath the plastic casing that holds a tremendous roll of institutional toilet paper is another sentence that appears to be part of the inflamed dialogue. It's written in the carelessly graceful script of someone who writes a lot by hand.

Hatred is futile,
and I'm sure they're not
too fond of you.

In capital letters to the right of these lines are the words

GO BACK TO YOUR
3RD WORLD AMERICAN FUNDED COUNTRY
YOU DICKHEAD

The writer of the next small public poem has returned to pencil over the whitened-out letters so that they remain clearly legible.

> America is strong enough
> to stand for those
> who stand against her.

I squat on the floor to study the wall, but no matter how hard I try to stare through the obscuring brushstrokes, the original message that inspired all of the fury and reflection doesn't materialize.

ADVISEMENT (JANUARY 23)

Though I can't recall her name, the student seated across the table seems familiar.

The art and design college where I teach teems with beautiful girls and boys, but this young woman with short red hair stands out among them. It's advising week. The cafeteria is packed with students waiting to see the professors who will help them choose their liberal-studies courses for the coming term. It's near the end of the first long day.

"Hello," says the girl. "I waited to see you because you took care of me last semester."

"I remember."

Vaguely, I do. I remember spending a long time helping her because she was worried about signing up for exactly the right courses. The almost visible tendrils of her anxiety are what come back to me now.

Glancing at her registration sheet, at the Russian polysyllables of her last name, the memory jells. She was worried about her English, which wasn't, she said, very strong. A young man came with her. Annoyingly, he did most of the talking on her behalf. Whenever he asked a question, I looked straight at her while I answered, as if he were merely acting as an interpreter.

"Do you know what you'd like to take?"

"I need," she says, as if she hasn't heard me, "sympathetic instructors. People who can understand."

"Understand what?"

"My fiancé worked on the hundred-first floor of the North Tower."

The eyes under her almond-shaped glasses film with tears.

"Oh," I murmur. "Oh, dear. I'm sorry."

"When I took my art history final last month, I couldn't remember anything. Nothing. Not one answer."

Tears drip down her cheeks. I glance around, but no one seems to notice. My colleagues flank me on both sides. Other students crowd close, waiting their turn. The room is abrasively public. If we were in my office, I could close the door and let her safely cry.

"I'm a good student," she's saying. "Until last semester—mostly B plusses and A's." She runs a hand through her cropped hair. Her nails are painted a luminous red. "That's not all. I got an e-mail saying he was alive and in a hospital, so I searched for him. I searched at two hundred hospitals."

"Two hundred?"

Her shoulders contract as if someone struck her. "It was terrible, the hope."

"Was the message signed?"

She shakes her head no.

"A cruel hoax."

And when the confusion in her eyes signals that she doesn't know the meaning of the English word "hoax," I say, "There are some very sick people in this world. I'm sorry you were hurt. Hurt more deeply, I mean."

She doesn't bother to wipe her cheeks. She must be so used to crying that it's become second nature.

"He was here with you last time."

She brightens. "You remember?"

"I remember that he was looking after you. I could see how much he cared."

"I can't believe you remember!"

Because memories are all that remain of him, I try to visualize him. The only detail I can summon is that he was tall.

The girl reaches into her purse, an elegant sling made of pale leather, for a tissue. Now we're able to discuss the course offerings. While I finish up the paperwork, I casually mention the counseling services that the university offers. It seems that she knows and has already availed herself of them.

"Thank you," she says, "for everything."

She rises from her chair, but I sense that she isn't ready to leave.

"Can I hug you?" I ask.

She nods. Half standing, I reach across the table to gingerly embrace her. Her shoulder blades feel as if they're made out of shell, and I want to rock her in my arms as if she were my own daughter. Just as badly, I want her to go.

Smiling encouragingly, I sit down again. The girl walks away without looking back. After a moment, I wave the next student in line over to me.

An Interesting Ontological Question (January 23)

When my mother calls with the news, my first thought is, it can't be true.

The reason it can't be true is because he's my father and because, according to the child's logic that comes alive whenever people I love are in danger, I haven't worried about him lately.

My father has just had emergency surgery to drain blood pooled on his brain, the result of a head wound from a fall in the bathroom. My mother says she's calling from the hospital in Santa Fe. I can see her standing at the bank of pay phones, lips pursed with anxiety.

We usually talk two or three times a week, conversations that center on cute-kid scenes every grandparent should know, like the time Gracie, dancing wildly around the apartment, sang out, "I'm exciting! I'm exciting!" Now I see that the idea of closeness created by the phone is illusory. I want to fly to New Mexico but am stopped by the idea of my daughter, who's still breastfeeding and who, if I take her along, will be a hindrance when it comes to hospital visits or my helping out. The miles gape between us. For the first time, I understand the helplessness my mother must have felt in the hours following the World Trade Center attack, especially after the land lines failed.

The next day, we talk again.

"Your brother's coming tomorrow," she says. "Don't worry, we'll be fine."

She then tells me a story. When the physical therapist visited my father in the hospital that morning, she asked him an array of questions meant to screen for possible brain damage.

"You know how deaf your father is," my mother says. "Well, he swears he heard the therapist say, `Do you kill a banana before you eat it?'"

"Do you kill a banana?" I echo.

"And do you know what he said?"

I nod into the receiver. Sometimes Gracie, unaware that the person on the other end can't see her, nods into the receiver, too. I wish I had a kid's easy faith, knowing the world conspires with your will. But faith or not, my father is recovering. This time he has survived.

"What did he say, Mom?"

"He said, `That's an interesting ontological question.'"

"An interesting ontological question?"

I laugh and, two thousand miles away, my mother laughs with me.

SUPERBOWL (FEBRUARY 3)

When the helicopter passes overhead, the apartment building's foundations shiver to the beat of the blades.

Gracie's eyes widen with delight. "Oh!" she says. "*Bu zhidao*? What is?"

"A helicopter," I tell her.

"Helicopter! In the sky!"

"See it?"

"My see it!"

The chopper now hovers a few blocks north, over the marchers protesting the World Economic Forum meeting in New York City. We saw evidence of the demonstration on our way home—not the protesters themselves but the flashing cherry lights of the dozens of squad cars gathered at the intersection of Second Avenue and St. Mark's Place. Gracie counted one, two, three, four vans packed with cops dressed in riot gear.

"We're living in a police state," Chuck muttered.

It's Sunday. All weekend long, the city has grown tense with the threat of more violence. The TV coverage of both the protests and the corporate forum that inspired them was sketchy, though. It felt strange to walk down streets filled with police cars and flashing lights, then turn on the television set to see models twirling on catwalks or talking heads calmly dissecting George W. Bush's State of the Union address.

After I put Gracie down to sleep for the night and finish preparing for Monday's classes, I realize how on edge I am. The days when I flinched at the sound of passing jets are over, but I'm still hyperalert to danger.

"All those cops today," I tell Chuck, who's next to me on the couch, watching the news. "It's become Us and Them again."

I want to say, but am too tired to shape the idea into words, that what I mean is that the demonstrations and the official reaction to them have obliterated the myth of a city united against an Enemy Other. Instead I lean back and try to concentrate on the book in my hands.

With the first explosion—a boom as loud as a close-range shotgun blast—Chuck springs up from the couch. When he walks over to the window, I wave for him to stand aside, so he's out of the line of fire.

There's a second boom, then a third. The sky above the schoolyard brightens with streaks of falling white light. Another rocket shoots high above the tenement roofs, leaving behind a trail of gray smoke.

Fireworks. The first fireworks since 9/11.

The Hell's Angels must be responsible. They occupy a building two blocks due south of us, on East Third Street.

Usually quiet neighbors, they set off fireworks in times of celebration. The Fourth of July. The World Series. The Super-bowl, which was held today. The Angels must be rejoicing at the results of the game. Someone must have won.

Adrenaline leaves a sour taste in my mouth.

And now a man is yelling. It takes me a moment to realize that George Bonafaccio, on the floor below, is screaming inaudible curses into the night.

As if the Angels might hear or care about his angry cries for peace.

PRAY FOR ME (FEBRUARY 9)

I'm wheeling Gracie home from a play date at Adeola's house when I see the sign. Hand-painted blue, it's posted on the door of one of the storefronts that are no longer stores but places where people live.

Sometimes I wonder what it would be like to live in a place that, by design, is an invitation to peer inside. Most store dwellers do their best to repel glances, but whoever lives here is obviously trying to draw them. The wide window isn't covered by the usual curtains, shutters, or Sleeping Beauty thickets of houseplants. Instead there's a movable rice-paper screen, the kind you sometimes see in home offices.

Gracie stares questioningly up at me.

"Just a sec, darling. Mommy has to read something."

The sign says: "Tell us what you need to pray for and we'll pray for you. Just fill out the form and put it in the mail slot with your donation."

"Mommy?" Gracie says.

"Soon, my patient girl."

Written in neat white letters on the window is a paragraph announcing that the two artists who live within are working to effect worldwide social change through mutual sharing.

Yeah, right, I think. What about the donation? You call that sharing? Possibly this is a kind of performance piece. In this strange era, no matter how hard I might hope otherwise, I can't believe the call to social change is sincere.

Gracie begins to climb out of her stroller. I've stopped strapping her in because she resists the restraints so passionately, and because she seems old enough to not need them. With freedom, each moment becomes an exercise in free will. The straps are inside you now, I tell her. They're in your mind.

"Okay, honey," I say. "We're out of here."

DREAMS (FEBRUARY 11)

The room is so bright because all of the walls are made of glass. Looking out, I see that we're above a layer of clouds. The ground below is invisible.

I'm on the 110th floor of the skyscraper they've built to replace the World Trade Center. The room I'm standing in isn't an office, however. It seems to be some kind of college dormitory, so stuffed with furniture there's barely enough room to navigate a path between the desks and beds to my bed, the one with the soft-looking comforter decorated with images of sea creatures.

The way the world is now, the sun no longer sets. I wonder how I'll manage to sleep in the eternal brilliance.

It's then I notice that I don't have a desk. Every bed but mine is paired with a sturdy wooden desk, a place to work.

The woman who materialized, the woman in charge, tells me that my desk is located many stories below. In dream language not spoken aloud, I ask her how I'll be able to write.

Also without moving her lips, the woman sternly tells me, "It's a burden many of us share. You are not alone."

The Year of the Horse

Today has been identified by the newly created Department of Homeland Security as a day to brace for terrorist attacks.

At ten in the morning, Liselot comes over with Adeola. While the girls play, we sit around the kitchen table talking. In a few minutes Liselot will go to work, Chuck will retreat to his office, and I'll head to school, leaving Gracie and Adeola in our baby-sitter Ping's care.

When Ping arrived an hour earlier, she gave Gracie a red envelope. In a red sky above a cityscape floated files of golden ideograms. The characters that loomed largest were the words for "good fortune." The rest I couldn't read.

While I stared at the envelope, the anonymous city resolved into New York, the skyline as seen from Battery Park. The World Trade towers were nowhere in sight. Shocked by the swiftness of the revision, I settled back on the rug to watch Ping help Gracie extract five one-dollar bills.

"All new money," she told me.

"Thank you. Say 'thank you,' Gracie. *Xiexie.*"

Transfixed, my daughter held a bill stretched before her face.

"And thanks for working on New Year's, Ping."

She shrugged. Her husband, who's getting a degree in computer science, would be in class till eight-thirty that night anyway. "Americans don't know about this day," she said.

I looked at the red envelope again. Hong Kong. The city on it wasn't New York but Hong Kong. I know grief creates ghosts, the dead friends or relatives you think you see walking down the street only to find you've seen strangers, but this was the first time the ghost was a whole city.

Liselot absently stirs her coffee with one of Gracie's purple spoons. She's saying that Adeyemi, her husband, spent most of yesterday preparing for the terrorists. He bought two cases of bottled water, latex gloves, canned food, and Army-quality gas masks for the whole family.

"He's ready," she says, laughing.

"I guess."

Chuck and I have been quick to call the terror alerts Republican ploys to keep the country cowering and bent to the White House's will. But what if we're wrong? Glancing through our long, narrow apartment, I spot the children at the other end. Both girls are staring at a dollar bill with the intensity of people witnessing a miracle.

Liselot wryly smiles. "If the bomb drops," she says, "you know where to find us."

ANNIVERSARY (FEBRUARY 12)

Tonight the Empire State Building isn't its now-customary red, white, and blue. The light-washed upper tiers are red and yellow, for red and gold, the celebratory colors of Chinese New Year.

This is the first night of the Year of the Horse. It's also Fat Tuesday and Lincoln's Birthday, the real birthday, not the ever-shifting bank holiday.

And it's the fourth anniversary of the death of our first baby. When I mentioned the fact to Chuck, a look of guarded concern flickered across his face and I knew he'd forgotten. So he wouldn't worry, I told him I was fine.

Now that he and Gracie are asleep, I can stare out the window at the tallest building left in our city and think about the fetal child who lived in me for five lunar months. All that remain of her are four black-and-white sonogram images showing a ferny spine and small skull with hollows for eyes. Scattered ashes. The memory of the first light tap-kicks.

In Natalie Angier's book *Woman: An Intimate Geography*, we're told that a woman carries her babies' cells in her bloodstream for perhaps the rest of her life. A mother thus is a "cellular chimera," a mosaic of her children and herself. She always has them inside her.

The body remembers. Mine is remembering now.

ON SALE (FEBRUARY 13)

At the checkout counter there's a cardboard-backed color photo of the World Trade Center. The glossy veneer makes the skyscrapers gleam. In the cloudless sky behind them hangs a see-through American flag.

A small sign above says, "On Sale $2.99." The original price, $3.99, has been crossed out by a single line that doesn't in any way obscure it, presumably so that customers, impressed by the markdown, might be tempted to buy.

Affixed to a piece of white cardboard below are a dozen or so lapel pins, the bronze-colored metal cast in the towers' image. A pair of American flags crossed like swords lies at their foundation.

In tiny letters at the very bottom are the words UNITED WE STAND.

VALENTINE'S DAY (FEBRUARY 14)

While the nurse prepares to draw blood to routinely test for anemia and lead poisoning, Gracie sits wrapped in my arms, wearing only her diaper.

"It's going to sting a little," I whisper, "but it won't last long."

Smiling brightly, the nurse, Doreen, jabs the needle fast and hard into Gracie's fingertip. A tremor passes through her body, but she doesn't cry. Instead she watches Doreen hold her pierced finger over a tiny glass vial. The drop that emerges is exactly the circumference of the vial's mouth. It fills it completely, a dark ruby.

More blood is needed for the second test.

"It's coming slowly because her hands are cold."

"Sorry," I say, and I *am* sorry I took Gracie to Union Square Park to play in the frozen sand if the torturously slow flow is the price.

"Let's warm those little fingers," Doreen says.

She rubs Gracie's plump hands between her two gloved ones. Blood smears the latex, and I remember the red-streaked caul the labor nurse held up for me to examine after the baby was born. She showed me the membrane because I'd asked to see it. I asked to see everything.

Soon enough, the blood starts to seep out. Gracie doesn't take her eyes from the drops collecting in a second, larger vial. Watching her watch, I feel a twinge of complicated pride. Would she be like me, someone so bent on the act of seeing that she forgets about pain?

"What color is your blood, honey?" I ask.

"Red."

"Red's the color of blood inside everyone."

"That's all." Doreen presses a square of cotton gauze to the fingertip. "Sorry to have tortured her, but the lab is very particular about there being enough. I'd hate to have to put her through this again."

No Possible Way (February 14)

In the evening, my mother calls to say my father must undergo a second round of surgery. They went to the hospital earlier because he was having trouble moving his legs and summoning words. The procedure to drain yet more blood pooled on his brain will begin within the hour.

"What did the doctor tell you?"

"We spoke for about two minutes. I'll call when he's out of recovery."

My mother's voice sounds tight and tired. She's not far from tears.

"How are you, Mom?"

"Not so good."

Since I already knew the answer, I'm not sure why I asked. We fall silent. I need to help her through the hours ahead but can't think of what to say.

It's my mother who speaks first.

"You know your dad," she tells me. "He was laughing all the way to pre-op."

After we hang up, I think about the ease with which my mother now employs the language of hospitals. *Recovery. Pre-op.* I wish I had thought to ask her what made my father laugh. What was the joke? What irony did he see?

He would have been seated in a wheelchair pushed by an attendant down a tiled corridor. The scars from his earlier surgery would still gleam. The first time around, they'd shaved the front half of his head. By now the hair would have grown in to a gray-black stubble.

"The only problem with this haircut is I look like Fu Manchu," he said over the phone a couple of weeks ago.

The memory of this joke will have to be enough to hold me— it and the faith that his ability to regard life from a slightly ironic distance will carry us through. Before he retired, he was an economist. If he taught me anything, it's that all known factors must be weighed. On September 11, while my mother hit redial again and again, desperately trying to get through to us, he dug out the Rand McNally map of New York, then calculated the precise distance between the World Trade Center and our apartment.

The towers, he announced, were 1.4 miles away. Even if they fell, and happened to fall to the northeast, there was no possible way that Jocelyn and her family could come to harm.

When I call the hospital the next day, my mother says, "He's watching *Wall Street Week*."

Though it's been years since he retired, my father still crunches the numbers. Knowing the economy's sinuous up and down turns is, after all, his way of understanding the world.

The first year I lived away from home, I visited him once in his corner office on the fortieth floor of the Marine Midland Building. New York Harbor glistened below. The newly completed World Trade towers loomed to the west. If we had been giants, we could have reached across vertiginous space to touch them.

He came out from behind his desk to hug me. The details are lost, buried under the crush of time, but I remember that we talked about Philippe Petit's tightrope walk between the two buildings. The greatest logistical problem to overcome, my father said, had been the wind.

In the restaurant he ordered me a beer, as if I were a real adult. The conversation focused on politics. I was grateful he didn't pry into my brand-new grown-up life. He knew how to stand back and let his children become what they were.

"How's he doing?" I ask my mother now.

"A few minutes ago he tried to explain the Enron scandal to me, but I couldn't follow," she says. "The problem wasn't him, it was me. Listening to us speak, you wouldn't know who'd just had the brain surgery."

In the laughter that follows, I hear her exhaustion and relief. Incomplete relief. The crisis is over, but it can come again. In the flash of a second, life's delicate sheath can burn away.

It's taken me until now to understand. I wonder how long she has known.

DEVOTIONS (FEBRUARY 20)

A blue sawhorse with the words "Police Line Do Not Cross" has appeared before the Ninth Precinct's 9/11 shrine.

No one from the station house died, so the display is a modest one. Two small American flags are taped to the limestone wall. There's a framed watercolor of the intact Lower

Manhattan skyline, and a page torn from a magazine with a photo of hard hats working the smoldering earth.

On the ledge sit three bud vases with three dried roses in them. A larger vase holds a bunch of cotton blossoms, the white tufts like the generic cotton balls you can buy at the Rite Aid on the corner. The water in which they sit is greenish black. Bands of dried scum near the lip mark what gradually evaporated over time.

The reason for the barricade is a mystery. Did someone try to defile the sad shrine? Is the sawhorse a deterrent, more symbolic than real, to potential vandals?

More likely it was placed there to stop the neighbors from their devotions. Maybe there was a mandate from above: no more bouquets, it's time to move on. Then again, maybe the cops are growing tired of the waning attention of the citizens around them.

Maybe the people they aid and arrest and interrogate have gone back to being just a job.

GHOSTS (FEBRUARY 21)

In the afternoon, while I'm playing tea party with Gracie, my old student Hyun Chul calls.

It's been almost a year since we spoke. I'm glad to hear from him. Hyun Chul and I have a complicated relationship colored by the fact that he sees me as a kind of mother and I see him as a kind of son. He seeks my advice at turning points in his life—when he came out, when he graduated, when he found a man he thought he could love.

He's a photographer. When I was nine months pregnant with Gracie, he spent a winter afternoon making a series of large-format images of me reclined on the couch against a dark backdrop of book-covered walls.

One picture from that session is a self-portrait of him curled at my knees. In it I twine my fingers through his long hair. My legs and belly are visible but not my face. It's impossible to tell whether the hand of the phantom mother seduces, punishes, or consoles.

Hyun Chul is calling because he doesn't know if he should quit his job managing a photo studio to go to grad school. He's worried because he has no real time to make pictures. In the year since graduation, a couple of his classmates already have found a measure of fame, and he's anxious about his own career. The problem is, if he works he can't shoot, and if he quits he'll be broke.

"Have you been taking any pictures at all?"

"On the weekends."

With an ominous look in her eyes, Gracie lifts a small green teacup into the air. "Drink, Mommy," she commands.

I touch a red cup to my lips. "Cheers."

"What?" Hyun Chul asks.

"The baby," I tell him. "We're pretending to eat and drink."

I ask if he's been to the World Trade Center site. His voice crackles, lost in cell-phone static. When I can hear him again he's saying, ". . . not my material. Besides I won't go down there until they build a memorial where you can leave an offering."

"That's good of you to want to show respect."

"I'm not just talking about respect," he says. "I'm talking about the ghosts. Think of all of those thousands of ghosts."

Despite his New York savvy, Hyun Chul remains an old-fashioned Korean boy. Unless you leave offerings—of money, food, flowers, whatever else might feed or appease them—the hungry ghosts will drag you down.

Gracie wraps her arms around my neck. Her skin smells of baby shampoo and milk. Staring at the tiny plastic dishes and cups, I think of the miniature portions of food set out to feed the ancestral ghosts every year during Qing Ming. What have 9/11's ghosts been fed? Votive candles. Wilted flowers. Thousands of fliers. Distant bombs, more death.

Changing the subject, I ask Hyun Chul if he's still seeing the man he thought he loved.

"No." He sighs with impatience or regret, I can't tell. "That ended ages ago."

Conspiracies (February 22)

The pizza that the waitress slides onto the table has two tomato-slice eyes with black olives for pupils. Another tomato slice cut into a half moon is the mouth. The nose is a piece of broccoli singed from the oven's heat.

"Oh, look!" Gracie cries.

Dublin bounces happily in the high chair next to hers. Lifting a pizza wedge onto a plate, his mother, Mairaid, cuts it in small pieces. I do the same. We're at Two Boots on Avenue A with our husbands and kids. The children have each other to play with, so the evening holds the promise of real adult conversation. Chuck and Eun Jin started talking right away. While Mairaid and I peeled off hats, scarves, mittens, coats, and snow pants, settled Gracie and Dublin into their chairs, and ordered the pizza face for them to share, I barely listened to what the men were saying. Now I'm ready to devote my full attention to the subject at hand.

"The original plot was hatched by the CIA under Kennedy," Eun Jin is saying.

Seeing the questioning look in my eyes, he explains that the plot called for the U.S. to blow up one of its own buildings, then pin the blame on Cuba.

"So they just took it out of the file and dusted it off."

Chuck nods as if this weren't the first time he's heard the idea. Mairaid absently stirs her tea. Of course she and Eun Jin would have gone over this ground before. I'm the only one who finds the theory startling.

"What evidence do you see?"

I've tried to guide my students away from the conspiracy theories flooding the Internet. In my freshmen class, we critically analyzed Nostradamus's purported prophesies before turning to Auden's "September 1, 1939"—the poem,

I told them, that made the e-mail rounds among my friends after 9/11.

Why are we searching for occult answers? I asked. Any halfway attentive reader of the news could have predicted another attack on U.S. soil. Why do we long for prophesies?

> All I have is a voice
> To undo the folded lie . . .

And I want to be wary of Eun Jin's and other conspiracy theories, but the truth is my need for answers hasn't been assuaged. While the attacks on the World Trade Center and Pentagon make perfect sense, a perfect retort to American hubris, the world power undone by a handful of men with box cutters, deep down I still can't grasp why we had to suffer.

"I know from growing up in D.C. that if any suspicious planes entered the airspace, the Air Force would be on them in a minute," Eun Jin is saying. "On the morning of nine-eleven, the command in charge of air surveillance was ordered to stand down for an hour. Exactly an hour. No one knows why."

"How do you know?"

"It's true there's been no investigation," Chuck says.

"Bush even told Congress not to investigate. Said we shouldn't divide the nation at a time like this. Pretty lame, if you ask me."

I take another sip of my beer. If I'm to be honest, no act of betrayal or subterfuge seems out of range. Watergate, a time of relative innocence, was just the beginning. Iran-Contra, stolen elections, a Supreme Court in collusion with the power that put it there . . . As the distance between what's said and what's done widens, a degree of collective madness has to set in.

Dublin grabs a tomato slice, then holds it over his mouth. Gracie claps her hands, delighted.

"Laughing!" she says. "Dublin's laughing!"

FEAR (FEBRUARY 26)

The American flag that hangs outside the Liberal Studies office snaps and hisses in the wind.

Whenever I hold office hours, I swivel the venetian blinds closed because I don't want my students—or anyone else, for that matter—to see me seated before the flapping flap. I want nothing to suggest that I approve of the fervor that has led to the bombing of Afghanistan, shadow governments, shredded treaties, and the imprisonment of innocent Arab men.

But I'm not holding office hours now, so the blind is pulled all the way up. Sunlight floods the room. Midday traffic on Fifth Avenue drifts past the Korean deli across the street, a view slashed by red and white stripes whenever the wind whips the flag high.

My task this afternoon is to review the journals from my creative-writing class. I enjoy leafing through student journals, admittedly not so much for the writing as for the sketches, paintings, collages, and photographs that accompany the writing. Sometimes the beauty of the images astounds me, and I'm proud to be teaching at such a good art and design school, a spontaneous pride I don't feel these days for my country.

The spiral-bound notebook lying open on my desk belongs to Dimitri, an illustration major who plays drums in a neo-punk band. Dimitri has kept his journal fairly religiously. Androgynous naked creatures drawn in a style somewhere between R. Crumb and Joan Miró people the pages. The thought and dialogue bubbles rising from their heads are crammed with tiny words written in a meticulous hand, meditations about jam sessions and hot girls and smoking 4 A.M. spliffs on subways in the Bronx.

Turning the page, I see two narrow columns of text placed side by side. A miniature prop plane circles one, leaving a trail of bubbles in its wake. Within the column-towers Dimitri has written: "For some reason planes were flying low over the city today. First one plane then another, flying so low. I was afraid. Very afraid. Very afraid. Very afraid."

The phrase "very afraid" is repeated over and over, forming the bulk of the buildings' bodies. I close the book. I remember the recent day of the low-flying planes, too. It was raining, and whenever the weather is bad enough to impair visibility, the planes flying into LaGuardia descend over Manhattan, straight across the city's heart.

THE WORLD (MARCH 7)

During Thursday's play date at Liselot's house, we take a few
minutes to catch up.

My friends have kept me sane through early motherhood,
which for all its joys has been a far busier, lonelier condition
than I'd imagined. Each week's play date comes as a relief. Like
writing, it's a way to step out of the daily rush, to believe that
life hasn't narrowed to squeeze out everything except
changing diapers and grading papers and hurrying between
work and home and the ten o'clock news.

Yvonne's period has finally started. She's glad not to be
pregnant again, especially now, in these ominous times.
Vicki is thinking of applying for a job as director of a
family clinic on the Lower East Side. Mairaid doesn't have
much to report except that Eun Jin, who works in adver-
tising, puts in so much overtime they rarely see him. The
economy being what it is, there have been layoffs at his
firm, and he's afraid to say no to the extra hours and be next
in line to go.

I tell them that my father might have to have brain surgery
again. At this point, it's too early to tell.

When Liselot's turn comes, she says, "Yemi and I need to
go out on a date. I think we've forgotten who the other
person is."

After we all offer to take Adeola for the evening, Liselot's
expression grows grim. "I have to say this also—I'm so

worried about the world. It's terrible. I can't even begin to talk about it."

Each day brings more news of death. The horror dominating the headlines now is in the Middle East. Later we will learn that on this day, at least twenty-five Palestinians were killed in a series of attacks by the Israeli army.

Until now we have passionately talked about almost every subject we've touched on. I've loved our conversations, and have learned from them. With the exception of Vicki, who, like me, is a U.S. citizen, my close mother friends are European women partnered with men born in Nigeria, Korea, and Iran.

Lately, though, I've grown uneasy about what divides us. Vicki is an observant Jew. When Yvonne married Adan, she converted to Islam.

"I know what you mean about the world," Vicki says now. "And I don't want to think of it this way, but sometimes I can't help feeling it's my people against theirs."

It's a moment before any of us can respond.

CARTOGRAPHY (MARCH 9)

Suddenly Gracie starts to howl. Within seconds her face is blotchy, bright with tears.

I kneel before the stroller. The slowly moving crowd on Fifth Avenue parts, then streams around us, as if our family were a small island that suddenly boiled into being in the middle of a river.

Soon the mystery of my daughter's distress is solved. Her mouth is crammed with raisins. There's no way she can chew and swallow them all.

"Spit some into my hand, sweetie."

I end up having to pry out the wet mass with my finger. Gracie's wailing grows louder. She's very tired. She and her father and I spent this warm late-winter Saturday at the Central Park Zoo. It's almost two hours past her nap time.

"Let's take a cab home," Chuck says.

He manages to hail one right away. When the turbaned driver sees the stroller, he pops open the trunk without having to be asked. Briefly I wonder if he, too, is the father of a young child.

Settled on my lap, Gracie stops crying. Instead of gazing out the window, which she loves to do whenever she's in a taxi or car, she stares at the map of New York City on the partition separating us from the driver.

Wedged between the map and the clear Plexiglas frame are several coins. Pennies, a couple of nickels, a quarter, a dime.

"Money," Gracie says.

The cab maps are intended for tourists, so I've never bothered to study them before. This one has the city's neighborhoods labeled and cleanly divided into pastel-tinted sectors. Landmarks have been drawn so that they appear to possess three dimensions. Sitting astride the flat city like Monopoly board-game pieces are a tiny Brooklyn Bridge and Washington Square arch, the golden Prometheus at Rockefeller Center, the Empire State Building.

The World Trade towers are the most crudely drawn, two gray slabs plunked down on the western edge of the Financial District. If the vibrations of the moving cab were to jiggle it lower, the nickel above them would cover them completely.

Looking up past the partition, I notice that an American flag decal, luminous in the afternoon glare, is stuck to the passenger side of the windshield. I've seen them in the windows of bodegas, delis, car service store fronts. For these small-business owners and the city's South Asian cabdrivers, the flags seem less a declaration of patriotism than a preemptive bid at self-defense.

The cab stops at the corner of East Fifth Street and Second Avenue. While Chuck takes the stroller out of the trunk, the driver—who, I think, must be a father—smiles and waves at Gracie, whose face now shines with her sunniest grin.

"Bye-bye, taxi," she says.

THE UNTHINKABLE (MARCH 9)

The news anchor, who looks as young as my students, says that the United States may bring atomic weapons to bear in the war on terror. A list of countries—nuclear powers and thus possible targets—flashes across the screen.

A second or two later, she moves on to another story.

"I can't believe this shit."

"It's a smokescreen," Chuck says. "I'm sure he'll back down."

"That he could even *say* it—"

"We don't really know who's doing the talking."

Black-and-white mushroom clouds blossom over Pacific atolls. Shadows that were people flash against the wall. School-children crouch under their desks, arms laced around their necks. The White House utterance so casually reported in the evening news brings the specter of nuclear annihilation back to life. It should have vanished with my childhood. It can't be haunting my daughter's now.

A commercial has come on. A blonde woman in Spandex running shorts stares at the lens while a voice-over in what's presumably her voice intones her secret desire to be true to herself. It could be an ad for athletic shoes, Internet servers, or new-model cars.

Still stunned, I stare at the screen. I'm not sure how we're meant to be manipulated, what it is we're supposed to be made to want to buy.

Six Months After

The TV screen holds the image of the gleaming World Trade towers against a clear blue sky. The roar in the background grows louder. For an instant, the dark shape of a plane can be seen against the North Tower's façade before it disappears in a booming black flame-pierced cloud.

"Holy shit!" a man cries.

In the days following September 11, Chuck and I and millions of others watched this footage again and again. Each time it felt new. But each time, without my realizing it, the sounds and visions sank deeper into my core, till my nerves knew the timing by heart. Bright towers, roar, plane, boom. Holy shit. The flawless sky beyond.

When I see the footage now, six months after the fact, my breathing remains deep and full. My pulse doesn't race. Tears don't form. The scene has become part of a documentary made by the French brothers who, in the middle of shooting what promised to be a small film about the lives of New York City firemen, found themselves in history's grip.

Some of the sequences are hard to watch. The most awful are of firemen standing in a darkened trade tower lobby while debris and ash rain down outside—a terrible rain punctuated by the gunfire thud of bodies shattering on the concrete.

New to me are the images from September 12. How little rubble there really was, how little was left behind. Incomprehensibly little. Recalling the first days wading through the wreckage, one fireman says, "You don't find a desk, you don't find a chair, you don't find a telephone, a computer. . . . The building collapsed to dust. How are we supposed to find anything if there's nothing left of the building?"

It's his incredulity—the incredulity of every one of the men who stand before the documentarians' lens—that breathes life back into a time not long in the past. *Holy shit.* I couldn't believe it either.

But now I'm no longer in shock. Everything replayed tonight—the plane crash, the buildings' fall, the fact of the more than three thousand dead in New York, Pennsylvania, and Washington, D.C.—everything seems possible. It happened, and I know it happened. It really happened.

And I wonder how I reached this point. How in half a year did I make a place inside myself for knowledge of a loss so large it was beyond understanding?

How did I come to believe?

Tribute of Light (March 11)

"Can you see them?" I ask.

I've just returned from the bedroom after nursing Gracie down to sleep. Chuck stands before the window, peering into the night. Looping my arms around his waist, I peer out with him.

Above the roof of the school across the street rise two faint blue shafts of light. The Tribute of Light. Without realizing it, I've been hungry to see these beams cast from the towers' foundations since hearing the news of their soon-to-be existence some days ago. But now that they're here, on the six-month anniversary of the World Trade Center's fall, they disappoint me. Is it because they're a little dim? Because they don't differ much from the klieg lights that sometimes flare above Manhattan? They *are* klieg lights, after all. I don't know what I was expecting.

"Cloud cover might be obscuring them," Chuck says.

Staring at the lights, I want them to be more than what they are. I want them to be brighter, a covenant in the sky, a vow to the end of violence.

It's then I notice that the beams shine farther to the west than the empty space the towers occupy in memory.

"I think they moved," I say. "Weren't they . . . ?" Instead of finishing the sentence, I wave both hands to the right, as if dismissing a bad idea.

Can I really have forgotten where the skyscrapers stood? For four years I saw them framed in this same window. They were part of the cityscape, part of my private idea of home. Can landmarks once so real be misremembered so soon?

"Yeah," says my husband. "I know what you mean."

IMAGINE (MARCH 13)

It's raining, cold, but the silver light glinting off the pavement means spring.

Crossing Lafayette Street on my way to school, I glance downtown. The top stories of the Tombs are wrapped in fog. The same soft veil would have covered the World Trade Center, too.

For a moment I allow myself to dream that under the rain-smoky darkness, lost to sight, the towers still exist.

NEIGHBORS (MARCH 14)

The picture of the American flag taped to Mary's front window has yellowed with age. The white stripes and stars have turned pale ochre brown.

Right after September 11, one of the tabloids, the *Post* or the *News*, printed a full-color flag on its back page so readers could do exactly what Mary did, clip it and Scotch-tape it to their windows. Several others in the neighborhood did the same, especially the Koreans and Pakistanis who own stores on the avenues.

Mary's flag is one of the few residential flags that remain. A widow in her eighties, Mary often leans on the sill to watch and call to neighbors walking by one story below. On her good days, face made up with bright lipstick and rouge, she slowly walks to the McDonald's on First Avenue for a cup of coffee. Osteoporosis has bent her back into the shape of a 7. Most of the times I see her, she's perched at her window.

"Hello, darling!" she calls whenever she sees Gracie. "I love you! You're my baby!"

Today, the day I notice her flag has darkened, Mary shouts her love as usual. But then she stops to correct herself.

"You're not really my baby, but I love you anyway."

Tilting the stroller up so that my daughter and downstairs neighbor can see each other, I ask, "How are you feeling, Mary?

The old woman's smile crumples into a frown.

"Oh, you know," she says. "The pain. Always the pain."

The Day Before St. Patrick's (March 16)

Rain threatens all morning but never comes. Though she's in a wild mood, Gracie rejects several offers to go outside and play.

"No, sweetie, that's dangerous. Get down."

Standing on top of the toilet tank, my daughter reaches for the framed 1950's photo of the naked woman that a friend unearthed while researching a scholarly book on porn. Nipples and vulva airbrushed into oblivion, the woman reclines on a lily pad, smiling at an unseen sky.

The thought materializes that if I just let Gracie fall, she'll never be tempted to climb the toilet again.

Shaken that I've allowed the thought to pass into consciousness—shaken, too, by how satisfying it feels—I hold out my arms.

"Jump to Mommy!

Grinning, Gracie turns, then leaps.

When she refuses to nap I carry her downstairs, plant her in the stroller, and pray that the fresh air and motion will lull her to sleep.

Outside it's another world. The cloud-darkened streets are packed with people. I'm surprised. These are by far the largest crowds I've seen since 9/11. During the past few months, our neighborhood has turned ghostly, frequented only by those of us who live and work here. The tourists and day-trippers disappeared.

But now they're back. In their body language and clothing and the way they bunch together in defensive groups, casting wary glances around them, I see New Jersey, Long Island, and Westchester slumming it in the gentrifying but still danger-tinged East Village.

Why have they descended on us now?

When I reach McSorley's on East Seventh Street, I understand. Waiting on line outside the famous pub are about a dozen white men and women. Three or four wear antennae with bobbing green cue-ball-sized globes on the ends. Others have on bright green hats that glow like radium in the prestorm gloom.

From the open door drift odors of spilled beer, damp wood, smoke. The city around us is braced for celebration, the first mindless spree in half a year. Tomorrow morning the streets will glitter with broken glass.

"Sleep," I murmur to Gracie. "Why won't you sleep?"

METAPHORS (MARCH 17)

Exhausted by the evening at Dore and Matti's house—while the grown-ups talked about Paul Celan, Afghanistan, and the possibility of nuclear war, she played with the dog and made towers out of dominos—Gracie falls asleep before we reach Second Avenue.

It's a misty night, the sky slung with low clouds.

What no one talked about, not in any depth, was Matti's recent heart attack. All Dore would say was that when friends called the hospital to ask how he was feeling, Matti answered, "Fine."

When I met Dore and Matti ten years ago, I was awed by the Rothkos and Motherwells on their walls, by the breadth of their collective knowledge, by the atmosphere in which they moved. They were true intellectuals. Compared to them, I was an undereducated child.

A decade older, I find their company sweet relief from the ordinary.

Chuck turns the stroller onto the avenue. "Matti looked so frail," he says softly.

The last time we saw him, Matti hadn't seemed old. His heart attack was a threshold he crossed. He has passed from then into now, into the presence of death.

In the downtown sky rise the two beams of light, which, according to the news, will shine all month long. Though they've shone for several nights running, tonight is the first time I've seen them from the street.

From our apartment window, the columns of light aren't particularly impressive. The window frame neatly encloses a partial view. Cut off, made domestic, the beams don't look monumental. They don't seem to stand for the lost towers.

But out here the light shafts look brighter. Reaching high above the city—much higher than the buildings they commemorate—they dead-end, stopped short by the clouds. They look like what they're supposed to be, ghosts of the destroyed skyscrapers, spirits traced in light.

Seen whole, the metaphor is complete.

PASSOVER (MARCH 27)

As might be expected, Seder at Ruby's is quiet this year.

September 11 and the daily news of death in the Middle East make celebration impossible. Local sorrows invade the table, too. Jane's mother's breast cancer has metastasized. Josie, one door down, is in the hospital with an inoperable brain tumor. Chuck and my friends Gina, Tom, and Shahid have been dead for less than a year. Each name is a prayer that lasts as long as it takes for the syllables to silently form.

"Don't forget Elijah," Ruby says when her son, Andrew, sets the wine bottle back down on the tablecloth.

Andrew lifts the bottle again, then pours a shot into a crystal goblet set in the center, near the matzos and bitter herbs. We raise our glasses, clink them together. Now is the moment when Andrew usually makes his Passover speech. He's a good speaker, graceful and profound. I look forward to his spiritual summations of the year.

But he's silent.

The silence is a pall that must be lifted, I feel. "Cheers," I say.

"Happy Passover," Andrew says.

"Dig in," says Ruby. "What's everyone waiting for?"

Later that night, after we put Gracie to bed and settle down to the news, we'll see the blasted I-beams and ashen interior of the hotel in Netanya where at least twenty people gathered for their Seder died in a suicide-bomber attack.

EASTER (MARCH 31)

The table before the altar is bright with daffodils dedicated to the dead.

Chuck and I squeeze into a pew with Liselot and Adeyemi. Our daughters aren't with us. A few minutes ago, we left them with Abdul in the nursery behind the sanctuary. Though it was her first time there, Gracie seemed fine. She waved good-bye and didn't look back.

So far, the day has been a sweet enactment of Christian childhood ritual. Gracie found all of the hidden eggs, then tore apart her Easter basket. Chocolate and yoke crumbs smeared her pajamas.

Gordon delivers a sermon well-pitched to his East Village congregation of semi-believers. Resurrection becomes a kind of metaphor, which makes it easier to accept, I suppose. I wish I could. Now more than ever, I long to believe in the miracle, feel the surge of new life and possibility. Without it, I'm not exactly sure how to go on.

After the service, Chuck emerges from the nursery holding Gracie. Her face is covered with mucus and tears.

"I missed Mommy and Daddy," she's saying. "I drank water and cried."

When I gather her into my arms, the double heaves of her heartbeat and sobs pound softly against my chest.

LONG WEEKEND (APRIL 13)

The frogs in the pond down the road fill the rainy night with their chirps. No trucks rumble down First Avenue. No helicopter blades beat above us; no car alarms or sirens blare from the street.

I'm unused to all the peace and quiet.

When we arrived at our cabin in Saugerties early this afternoon, Gracie demanded that we return to her city. Pining for the life she believes is gone forever, she fell asleep at 3 P.M. Six hours later she hasn't awakened. At this rate, she'll be down for the night.

Chuck lies on the couch reading. I'm at the green table we salvaged from the East Fifth Street trash, writing and leafing self-indulgently through Yeats. *Peace comes dropping slow.* I'm glad to be here but, like my daughter, am dogged by a sense of loss. The loss may have to do with relaxing, letting go. All tension is gone. The almost inaudible murmur of grief that's been background music for months has faded to silence.

And it dawns on me that I'm mourning the loss of mourning. Sorrow has carved a home inside me. For seven long months I've carried its warm weight, which filled me like love. Like love, it was what I dreamed my way back to whenever I could. And though I know better, I can't help believing that sorrow links us to the dead. In a way, grieving helps keep them alive. They need us.

"Are you done?" Chuck asks.

Looking into his eyes, I see how tired he is. We're all exhausted. It's time to turn off the lights and, wrapped in the country's almost total darkness, fall asleep.

SAFETY (APRIL 14)

Overnight it has become summer.

Back in the city, Tompkins Square Park is loud with children. Across the playground I spot Jane, whom I recognize by the red hair and the infant strapped to her chest. She's pushing her three-and-a-half-year-old, Elena, on one of the tire swings.

"Does Gracie want to swing, too?" Jane asks me.

In answer, my daughter gravely nods. Soon she's flying with Elena in arcs above the blacktop. Her small hands circle the chains. She's swinging higher—much higher—than she's ever done before.

Eyes fixed on her boneless-looking wrists, I'm poised to dive in and save her. Gradually, though, I see how well she's holding on. Relief and loss hold me in a complicated embrace. My little girl is growing up.

After I admire the baby, who's seven months old, I tell Jane about our weekend in the country. The peacefulness. The sense of relief.

"Did you know we're thinking about leaving the city?" she says. "New York is a target. It's only a matter of time. If we stay we might live—or not live—to regret it."

Stepping closer to the hurtling tire, I take over pushing.

"When we were upstate this weekend, we met a man with three children," I tell her. "On September 12 he moved his family from Tribeca to Woodstock." It was as if they fled, I add. Not as if. They did.

"Nice if you can afford it," Jane says.

Glancing at the girls, I say, "Two hands, Gracie. The rule is you have to hold on with two hands."

She returns the strayed hand to the chain.

"But you know," Jane says, "Woodstock's within fallout range of Indian Point, isn't it? So it's not safe either."

Where is? I think. Jane lightly rubs her baby's fine red hair, over the place where the fontanel was before the small skull hardened closed.

NATURAL HISTORY (APRIL 20)

The apartment building begins to tremble.

Trembling is nothing new. Every time a heavily loaded truck drives by on First Avenue, a shiver passes through the foundations. What *is* new is that instead of fading, the trembling grows stronger. The couch I'm sitting on with my daughter lifts and dips like a rubber raft on rippling waves.

I'm frightened, but Gracie slept badly the night before, so it's a tired kind of fear. I call to my husband, who's in the kitchen fixing me a birthday breakfast. Gracie looks up, then goes back to shredding the tissue paper that enfolded my gifts, a pair of black capris, three G-strings, and a new translation of *The Tale of Genji*.

"Chuck!" I yell again.

According to the latest color code for disaster, the Northeast is under a yellow alert for terrorism. Do rocking waves mean terror?

The motion subsides.

When Chuck walks back in, I say, "Didn't you hear me?"

"No." He hands me a plate of scrambled eggs, and I forget to ask if he felt the waves, too.

An hour later my mother calls to wish me a happy birthday
and see how we survived the earthquake.

"Five-point-two on the Richter scale," she says. "Not much,
but enough to do some damage." She grew up in Southern
California and knows about real earthquakes. Still, she couldn't
help being a little worried.

"You remember what Manhattan's made of," I tell her.
"Bedrock. We're okay."

Since it's raining, we ditch our plans for the zoo and instead
go to the Museum of Natural History.

The herd of elephants that stampeded through my childhood dreams still divides the vast room. The dimly lit Hall of
African Mammals is crowded with families. This is Gracie's first
time here. Chuck and I want to show her the dioramas of animals standing before their painted backdrops of deserts, forests,
and mountains. Born and bred New Yorkers, we remember the
dioramas as magical.

Only now the tableaus are heartbreaking. Glass eyes hazy
with dust, the antelopes, lions, and gorillas shot by Teddy
Roosevelt and other big-game hunters seem flea-bitten and
unequivocally dead. The mothers are posed so that they
nurse or cradle their young. The fathers watchfully stand guard.

It's a relief when we discover the half-hidden exhibit
devoted to the natural history of New York City.

Most of the animals in the room are still alive. Carp, turtles,
garter snakes, praying mantises, ladybugs, and frogs writhe or

swim or hold as still as stones in their aquariums and cages. The exhibit also includes material on the city's geology. While Chuck helps Gracie aim a smudged magnifying glass at a salamander, I scan the legends under the title "New York in the Making."

The New York area was once covered with glaciers, I read, pleased to encounter words that confirm what I already know.

Then my eyes fall on the black-and-white illustration of the twin towers. A frozen gray river bears down on the skyscrapers rising in its path. The tops of both buildings have been whitened out, as if someone tried to scratch the images away.

The snow and ice of the glaciers was more than a thousand feet thick, almost as tall as the World Trade Center. When the glaciers melted, they left behind

Glacial striations	or scratches and grooves formed in the bedrock by rocks and ice moving over it
Glacial deposits	or the rocks left behind, which formed new land
Glacial erratics	or boulders standing alone

Looking again at the incompletely erased towers, I wonder how the display's creators could have thought the buildings had the enduring presence necessary for them to serve as a comparison to something embedded in geological time.

When the World Trade towers fell, the tremors that shook the island's core faded before they could reach us. What will be left when the last person touched by the disaster is finally gone?

Looking down, I see Gracie in her purple dress trying to scale the boulder that's on display because of the striations that score its glittering face.

"Hi there, sweetheart." Dropping one hand, I stroke my daughter's soft hair.

VOLATILE CHEMICALS (APRIL 25)

Unable to move any real distance without a walker or wheelchair, my mother-in-law, who spends most of her waking hours before the television, is the first to call.

"Are you all right?"

She doesn't say, "Hi, this is Ma," her usual greeting. Though I recognize her voice, it takes me a second to realize who it is.

"We're fine, Ann. How are you?"

"You sure?"

"I'm sure."

The sky beyond the window is dark with rain. I glance at my watch. In five minutes I'll have to start walking to school. I don't teach today, but there's a committee meeting I should attend.

"Didn't you hear? Thank God Ed's okay."

Ed, my brother-in-law, lives across town in Chelsea. The veins in my temples pulse. The dread that's always waiting just below the skin of consciousness shimmers to the surface. It's happening again.

"Wait a sec, Ann, I'm turning on the TV." If there are answers to be had, they'll appear on the screen.

The image crackling into focus is of several men sitting side by side on a city curb. Their eyes are blank. White sheets or blankets enfold their shoulders. Two of them have bandages or cloths wrapped around their heads. There's no sign of blood.

The men might be Middle Eastern or Latino. The city in the background might be any city, but because my mother-in-law's voice is sharp with anxiety, it must be New York.

"What happened?" I murmur.

Hearing the television, Gracie races into the room, followed by Ping.

"I don't want her to see this," I tell Ping. "Can you try to keep her away?"

"What?" says Ann.

"Watch a little!" Gracie hollers.

"No, honey."

"Watch!"

Chuck wanders in from his office, where he's been trying to write. I hand him the phone, then lift our daughter into my arms.

"I know you want to, sweetie, but you can't. Not now."

She wraps her arms around my neck. Over the past few weeks, my departures have grown heartrending. Every time I leave for school, Gracie cries as if I were leaving forever.

Cupping the back of her head, I swing around in a half circle so I'm the one facing the screen.

"Who is it?" Chuck is saying. "What is it?"

"Your mother. An explosion of some kind."

"Oh shit."

We fall silent. The only sounds are the anchorman's voice and the rain now lashing the windowpane.

"Ma?" says Chuck.

I stare at the set, see the shattered glass, the debris-littered street, the injured men waiting to be taken away.

"This can't be happening."

This can't be happening, a meaningless phrase people recite whenever what they're afraid of comes again. It can be happening, is happening. The latest news is entirely believable.

"Nineteenth and Fifth," Chuck says, naming an intersection six blocks north of my office. "Why don't you stay home?"

Later we'll learn that the explosion, which injured more than a dozen people, probably was caused by volatile chemicals stored in a basement. Relatively little damage was done. In any other year, the blast would have been a blip on the screen, a thirty-second spot on the local evening news.

"No, Ma, she's not going anywhere," Chuck says.

He's not trying to dictate my actions, he's only trying to keep his mother calm. *She's not going anywhere.* I think of the rain, the nodding heads around the conference table, Gracie's inevitable tears.

Smiling at her, I say, "That's right, honey. Mommy's not going anywhere. Today I'm staying home."

TRANSFORMATIONS (MAY 3)

Across from me in the car on the Brooklyn-bound F train sits a woman or girl—I can't get a fix on her age—who's wearing an American flag T-shirt.

Flags have grown common in these shrilly patriotic times, so the image alone isn't what draws my eye. This one's colors are mottled, faded. Ghostly figures slide through the pale red stripes and field of stars. This flag resembles Jasper Johns's famous painting, the one of the U.S. flag half buried by layers of white encaustic. I've always loved the painting, a perfect image for its time, and maybe this one, too, the flag almost invisible under all that white, the struggle to persist tragic and beautiful, the artist's eye ennobling but cool.

Golden hoops fluted into figure eights hang from the woman's earlobes. Art or protest doesn't seem to be her intent. I can imagine her sorting laundry at the end of the day, after work or school is over. The silk-screened shirt could easily have landed in the whites pile by mistake. A single dose of bleach would have been enough to soften the flag's strident primary colors into their current phantasmal shades.

When the subway doors slide open at Broadway-Lafayette, she rises to leave.

Was the shirt a gift? A giveaway? A deliberate purchase? Is

wearing it a declaration of allegiance or support for the war on terror? What does it mean to her?

Maybe nothing. Maybe the flag is simply a decoration, like a sunflower or rainbow or stars and moon.

THE ACUTE PHASE (MAY 4)

The voice projecting into the room belongs to Sharon.

Gracie has just gone down for her afternoon nap. Ordinarily I'd let the answering machine finish the job of taking the call so I could write, but Sharon is pregnant again, and I want to hear every drop of news.

I've followed the passage of her seasons almost as closely as I would if I were the pregnant one, my excitement for her tinged by my ambivalent longing for another child. Sharon is in her nineteenth week, almost halfway home.

"How are you feeling?"

Even before she tells me, I hear in her voice what's wrong. She has lost the baby, which was—was to have been—a boy. We talk for a solid hour, our longest unbroken conversation since Gracie and Jack were born. Listening to her, I realize she'll get through this. She's a strong woman, able to face pain without giving in to the temptation to wallow in it.

Three days later Sharon e-mails me. "I am being careful not to speed too quickly back to normal," she writes. "There is something about the acute phase that's precious, that you don't get back."

Yes. Through grief's liquid lens the world can shine with unbearable beauty. Certain objects—a tulip petal, a broken cup, a hand resting on a table—glow with significance. All things swell with meaning, become interconnected. In this respect grieving isn't unlike writing, being in the grip of a long narrative as it nears its end. I imagine it's like mystical transport, too, like feeling God's breath in the wind.

When the world glistens with grief's electric colors, the dead seem to be with us. They're brought to life. They're almost here.

After the acute phase is over, all that's left of them is memory.

ENDINGS

Neighbors (May 16)

A week has gone by since the Ninth Precinct moved away from East Fifth Street to a station house on Avenue C.

For days leading up to the move, an industrial-sized dumpster outside the police station slowly filled with dented filing cabinets, broken office chairs, and black plastic bags of garbage. Now it and the angled line of squad cars are gone. A piece of orange construction paper with the precinct's new address is stuck by strips of duct tape to the heavy wooden door.

Without the usual activity and noise, the block feels empty. Abandoned. Someone has placed a vase with a dozen white roses on the top step of the stoop. Looming over the flowers is a large Easter bunny with a silken pink nose.

I find myself missing the cops, too. After September 11 the veil of mutual indifference perpetually hanging between us burned away. Instead of ignoring each other when we passed on the street, we all nodded or said, "Hello."

After all these years together, we became neighbors.

PROUD TO BE AN AMERICAN (MAY 8)

The island of shelves that usually holds seasonal items like Christmas wreaths and jack-o'-lanterns is stacked high with electric American flags that, their boxes proclaim, are lit by one hundred fifty miniature lights.

We're here at Kmart this wet Saturday afternoon to kill time. Chuck and I select a rubber bath mat and a beige bathroom rug. Gracie chooses a dozen thumb-sized glow-in-the-dark dinosaurs. Shopping done, we head to the upstairs cafeteria for milk and cookies, the sugary treat a consolation for the rain.

The cafeteria's half-moon windows face downtown. Staring out at Lafayette Street below, I remember the column of smoke, the slow river of Financial District refugees. For a second, before it dissolves back into memory, I can actually see a ghost image of the dark, disjointed parade.

"Careful, honey," I murmur the moment before Gracie spills her milk. We all watch it spread over the table in a smooth white fan.

While Chuck waits on line, I push the stroller through Accessories in an attempt to distract our daughter into sitting still.

Once again we pass the island with the electric flags. This time I notice other products as well, twig wreaths festooned with fake roses and U.S. flags, carved eagles whose talons grip signs reading "Home of the Free" and "United We Stand." An Uncle Sam cradles two oversized stars. Stretched above his head is a red, white, and blue rainbow etched with the words "These Colors Don't Run."

I can't imagine New Yorkers actually buying 9/11 memorabilia, if that's what this kitsch can be called. None of it interests Gracie, so I take her around to the other side of the island, the only side we haven't yet seen.

There, we encounter a wall of plush teddy bears. The bears stand in a pyramid of open-faced boxes rising almost to the fluorescent lights. They're wearing uniforms: police uniforms, army fatigues, firefighters' protective gear.

On each box is written, "I sing 'God Bless the U.S.A.'"

Reaching over, I squeeze a fireman bear on the paw. A chorus of male voices erupts from the bear's torso. Most of the lyrics elude me, but I make out a repeating phrase that must be the chorus: "I'm proud to be an American."

Then it's over. A single voice that sounds suspiciously like George Bush's intones, "God bless America."

Unable to believe what I've heard, I squeeze the paw again, and again the jaunty song rumbles from the bear's belly. And I wish I could laugh. I wish I could feel cynical and superior, immune to the unholy toys before me, but instead my eyes fill with angry tears.

Gracie grabs a bear near her.

"No! Don't touch it!"

Afraid she'll think the anger is aimed at her, I push the stroller toward the registers, where Chuck is waiting to pay. Glancing back, I see a woman with a wine-colored birthmark covering one cheek lean close to a bear to examine the price.

TALKING ABOUT THE STARS (MAY 24)

Gracie and I are turning over slabs of shale in search of bugs. The sky is a cloudless blue. The air smells of pine needles and new grass.

It's our fifth day here at our place in the country. Tomorrow afternoon we'll drive back down to the haze-shrouded city, on the first leg of a trip to New Mexico to visit my parents. I'm just beginning to relax and don't want to leave.

When I look up, Miranda is walking across the meadow with a large earthenware jug in her arms. For the past year she's been squatting in the abandoned sleep-away camp down the road. She lives in one of the tilting frame bungalows, bathes in the stream, and harvests nettles, mushrooms, and berries to supplement what she can forage from the free bin in the health-food store in Saugerties.

Setting down the jug, Miranda hugs me, then shyly waves hello to Gracie. I haven't seen her since last summer. Her trousers and blouse hang loosely around her body. She's clearly lost weight.

Gracie continues searching for bugs. After a while, she solemnly stares up at us. "Look what I have," she says.

We peer down at the bright green caterpillar clinging to her index finger.

"Good work," I tell her. "What a good bug finder you are. But remember to be gentle. Bugs are little, and you are big."

"I'm a big girl."

"You're leaving soon?" Miranda asks me.

"Tomorrow."

"Tomorrow? Oh my God! What an intense time to travel."

Thinking she's alluding to the reports of new terrorist threats, I say that the news is overblown, the White House's attempt to control us through fear.

"Oh," says Miranda, "I don't know anything about that. I was talking about the stars."

The stars?

The stars and planets are aligned in a way that's as portentous as just before September 11.

"There's a full moon, too," she adds. "The first of the season."

Anxiety clouds her young, open face. Remembering herself, she forces a laugh. "Don't worry, though. Probably nothing will happen to you."

I smile back at her, to reassure us both. "The chances," I say, "seem pretty slim."

9/11 DOG (MAY 25)

We have sublet the apartment for the summer, so we arrange to sleep at Joan's loft near the Bowery, an easy drive to the airport for our early morning flight.

Gracie falls in love with Joan's new dog, Goldie, a gentle wheaten terrier who lets her tug the stump of her tail and pet her on the nose.

Watching the child and dog lie side by side on the floor, I tell Joan I feel in my bones that Goldie won't snap or do anything unpredictable. "My mother antennae don't go up with her at all."

Joan scoops more coconut sorbet into a porcelain bowl with blue goldfish glazed on the sides. "She's very sweet with children," she says. "When I walk her, she goes up to every stroller she sees."

Goldie is a pound dog. Unlike other pound dogs I've known, she lacks the skittishness of an animal molded by fear. Joan adopted her in January. When Goldie was taken into the shelter in December, she weighed a skeletal twenty pounds. Since then she's gained eight pounds but is still skinny.

"As a street dog, she was a real failure." Joan glances at her pet, who has rolled over so that Gracie can rest her head on her belly. "Clearly her old owners took good care of her."

She passes the dessert container to me. "I have a theory about her. I think she's a 9/11 dog. In the confusion of the first days, she got lost."

"Well, she's wonderful," I say. "I'm glad you found her."

I imagine Goldie, answering to a name we'll never know, padding through the ash-covered streets, sniffing the acrid air for signs of a family that never came home.

"She's thriving now," Joan is saying, "but you should have seen her. No one knew how close to starvation she really was."

SECURITY (MAY 26)

The airport on Long Island offering the cheapest fares to Albuquerque is so small that several prop planes are tied down to the tarmac at our gate.

Security, though, is tight. Chuck and I must produce photo ID's every step of the way. A uniformed man wearing latex gloves switches on Chuck's laptop, then mine. He and the other screeners seem serious about their jobs. The woman at the X-ray machine really looks at the objects suspended in our carry-on luggage. I wonder what she thinks about the contents of the pink knapsack Gracie packed herself: an uninflated blue balloon, a single maraca, and a beaded purse jammed tight with glow-in-the-dark dinosaurs.

If this year were like any other, we would have flown to New Mexico for the previous Thanksgiving or Christmas. But this year is not like any other. The idea of flying with my family so soon after September 11 paralyzed me. Though the worst of the paralysis is gone, I'm still not unafraid.

Before boarding, we must show our ID's yet again. Lined up with the other pre-boarders—small children and their parents, for the most part—I watch an elderly man in green Bermuda shorts lower himself onto a folding chair. He slowly, painfully, removes his sandals, then, lacing both hands under one knee, lifts his thin leg so that the screener can pass the wand of a metal detector over his white-socked sole.

Because Gracie is watching, I say to her, "They're looking carefully at the man so we can be safe."

The moment the words leave my mouth, I realize how little sense they make—to Gracie and to us all.

Memorial Day (May 27)

The thunderheads rising above the Sangre de Cristo Mountains look like atomic clouds.

Sitting near the picture window in the living room, my father watches Gracie roll bits of Play-Doh into snakes and worms. The scars on his head are bright pink, the ruptured muscle underneath healing in smooth ripples like the inside of a seashell. He's doing so well, my mother says, because of daily applications of liquid Vitamin E. But he seems drawn into himself, as if all of his energy were devoted to healing, which maybe it is.

Chuck walks in with a fresh mug of coffee. It's about ten-thirty in the morning.

Suddenly an F-16 roars through the sky. The skin on my throat tingles. Going over to the window, I anxiously scan the cumulous clouds but see no trace of the fighter jet's vapor trail.

"Memorial Day," I murmur to my husband. "Must be an aerial display."

Kirtland Air Force Base is sixty miles to the south, right next to the airport in Albuquerque. Sometimes civilian planes taxi so close to the base, passengers can see camouflage-painted choppers, the slender black bodies of stealth fighter planes.

My mother emerges from the bedroom, her hair damp from the shower. Like my father, she's completely unperturbed by the jet's roar. For them the plane's thunderous passage was as innocent a sound as the stutter of a semitrailer's Jake brakes on St. Francis Drive.

Chuck meets my eyes, nods.

Turning to his parents-in-law, he points to the sky, then says, "In New York, that sound means trouble."

THE FINAL PIECE (MAY 29)

Strands of heat rise from the parking lot, but under the outdoor café's *portal* it's shady and cool. I have escaped from my parents' crowded house for an hour to read the paper and hear myself think.

On the front page of the national edition of the *New York Times* is a color photo of an I-beam being lowered by crane onto a flatbed truck. A crowd of construction workers in hard hats and reflective vests looks on.

Letters and numbers can be seen on the scorched steel surface. NYPD 23. FDNY 343. They are, I realize, tallies of the dead. The beam, I read, once supported the South Tower. It is the final piece of debris to be removed from Ground Zero.

Thirty-seven weeks have passed since September 11. During that time, more than a million and a half tons of wreckage and nearly twenty thousand body parts were removed from the site. The grim work is over.

Folding the newspaper, I lay it on the metal table. Sunlight glancing off the bumper of a passing pickup blinds me. Shielding my eyes, I wish we'd never left the city. I want to be, long to be, back in New York for this moment.

And it's a strange, sad longing, as if for a lover I haven't seen in years—someone who, I've learned from friends of friends, has recently died.

SHADOW FUNERAL (MAY 31)

The sweet scent of Russian olive trees in bloom fills the night air. I'm sitting alone under my parents' *portal*. In the house behind, the people most tightly bound to me by love, blood, and need are sound asleep.

A second-day photo of the South Tower beam stretches across the *Times*'s front page. The steel is now covered with black muslin, an American flag, and a funeral wreath.

When I glanced at the image this morning, it disturbed me, though I couldn't say why. In the few minutes before sleep, I want to get to the bottom of my disquietude.

The way it's being revered, the beam could be a coffin holding the tremendous body of a war hero or head of state. Unsettling as it may be, the solemn pomp makes a kind of sense. There's no real corpse to mourn—not enough of them, anyway. In a terrible act of transubstantiation more than 2,800 people were made one with the debris. The final beam is a piece of the True Cross.

This isn't the whole answer, though. A cat streaks across the garden wall. The scent of blossoms grows stronger, and now I'm remembering all those weeks we breathed the burned air. I couldn't bear to think about it then, but now I can say we were breathing in the dead. We breathed their ashes. Their vaporized bodies became a part of us. They're part of me and Chuck and Gracie, part of our neighbors, part of the tens of thousands like us who live or work or go to school in Lower Manhattan. We carry the dead inside us. Even after our bodies slough off the physical traces, they'll still be there.

Shadow funerals can't do the trick. There's no way to say good-bye, no way to bury the dead in us.

DREAMS (JUNE 2)

From the mouth of our cave, the Hudson River looks like molten gold. A helicopter circles, dips low.

I pray the pilot hasn't spotted us.

Like most who still live in the city, Chuck and I have taken refuge in the caves under the West Side Highway, which provide shelter from the strafing runs and bombs.

Chuck says that the pilot *has* seen us, that our hiding place is no longer secure. We decide to walk with Gracie to the country, but when we get there a moment later we realize that our country house isn't safe either. Our neighbors might inform on us. It seems safer to camp in the woods.

Because I desperately need to take a shower and fetch clean socks for Gracie, I venture into the cabin. On entering the darkened rooms, I quickly pull off my clothes. But when I remove my blouse, a second one appears underneath. Under that one, there's another. Like a bag lady, I'm wearing layer upon layer. I unbutton buttons, tug at zippers. Panic builds. I'll never be naked, never finish what I set out to do.

And now a neighbor's shadowed face presses against the window. I have been identified.

Wedding Day (June 3)

"Take a look at this," Chuck says.

He lifts our wedding picture from my parents' bookshelf, then settles next to me on the couch. The photo is an eight-by-ten color enlargement of us standing on the Brooklyn Bridge, an image so familiar I stopped looking at it years ago.

"Here," he says. "See?"

In the background rises a single out-of-focus tower of the World Trade Center. Its twin is hidden from view by one of the bridge's piers. The pier's gray stones seem solid and real; the skyscraper dissolving in the August haze is a mirage.

After the slight shock fades, I study the two of us. The first thing I notice is how young and slim we are. Chuck wears his lucky Cub Scout belt buckle and light blue shirt with the sleeves rolled up; I have on my white minidress. His arm is draped around my shoulders. We've both taken our glasses off. Smiling, we stare myopically in the direction of the camera.

The wedding took place nine years ago at City Hall. After the brief ceremony, witnessed by our closest friends, Andrew and Gina, we all walked to the midpoint of the Brooklyn Bridge, where this picture was taken.

The summer morning was humid and hot. Gina wore jeans with a hole torn in one knee. Of all my friends, Gina would have known what to think of September 11. I kept wanting, and keep wanting, to call her. But, like the towers, she's gone. She died of breast cancer last April. She never knew about the attacks on the World Trade Center towers and the Pentagon, never knew about Afghanistan. She was too good for this time, I said to myself soon after 9/11, realizing even then the idea was born from the mild derangement of loss. Still, it's true. Though she'd laugh if she heard me think it, she was too good for the fallen world.

Fallen world? she'd say. It fell long ago, and besides, when was it ever Eden?

Willing sadness away, I tap the tower's image and say, "Which one do you think it is?"

It seems important to know, to pin down, name the tower that has intruded into the image marking the start of our life together—that's been there all along, waiting to be destroyed.

The building lacks an antenna, or seems to. In the haze and enlargement's graininess, it's impossible to tell for sure.

"Let's see," Chuck says. "The North Tower was the one farthest to the west, so this must be the South Tower."

We both stare at the photograph of our younger selves—two people wildly in love who didn't yet know what it meant to share a life—standing before a pale skyscraper that now exists only in pictures.

WITNESSES (JUNE 3)

One of the slides at Salvador Perez Playground is made of plastic rolling pins that whirl in unison as each child flies down.

Gracie opens her legs in a V. As she descends, the spinning pins make a sound like pebbles falling through a rain stick. Though the slide is steep, she didn't hesitate for a second. Stationed at the bottom, I'm amazed by how grown-up she seems. Over the past few weeks, she has elongated and slimmed down into a creature who can no longer rightfully be called a baby.

A woman standing near me says, "You'd think that thing would cure cellulite, but I can tell you from experience it doesn't."

She's wearing overalls and wire-rimmed glasses. Like me, she's an older mother for so young a child. Her name is Lina. While we talk, Lina's daughter, Marta, consents to play with Gracie, even though she's her junior by a year.

It turns out that, like my Wisconsin friend Sharon, Lina is an art historian, a curator at one of Santa Fe's museums. Soon we're talking passionately about writing, art, motherhood, work. The sun climbs higher, driving us into the shadows beneath the castle turrets, where Gracie and Marta take turns burying each other's then our legs in the cool sand.

The talk shifts to September 11. In all my conversations on this trip so far, the subject inevitably comes up. A slight awkwardness overcomes those who ask. They're curious to hear about my experience, but they don't want to commit a faux pas by probing, touching exposed nerves. I think of the cautious way people can ask after the health of not-so-close friends who've got cancer or have tested positive for HIV. In the eyes of those who weren't there, I'm a survivor.

"What did you think of the news coverage?" Lina asks. She goes on to say that she was outraged by the canned footage of the anti-American Palestinian protests CNN aired soon after the attacks.

"It was so false, so slanted, so inflammatory I had to turn the TV off," she says.

I'd forgotten about the fallout from the controversial footage, which I didn't see because we'd stayed tuned to the more detailed local news. While Lina and I parse CNN's sins, I drift back to the days right after September 11, the hours Chuck and I spent sitting before the set. Lina's decision to turn it off wasn't an option. I needed to watch. I needed answers. I needed to hear about the rescues and then, when they didn't materialize, keep tabs on the shifting, horrific tallies of the missing and dead. I needed to see the towers burn and fall over and over again.

Nine months later, I still can't name the root of my need. It has something to do with the way a child picks at a scab, each fresh flow of blood confirming the fact of the wound. Lina and the others are wrong: I'm not a survivor, I'm a witness. What I hadn't realized before is how much pain a witness can and must feel.

At a few minutes before noon Lina and I get up, brush ourselves off, gather our sandy daughters, pails, shovels, and bags, and head for the parking lot. We exchange phone numbers, a gesture that says we enjoyed each other's company. Between my parents and old friends, I doubt I'll have time to call.

Conversation (June 11)

They've gotten dressed up for the restaurant, my father wearing a red Western shirt and bolo tie, my mother an embroidered vest with tiny mirrors sewn in. I'm relieved to see they've made the effort, which means they're returning to themselves.

For the first time since our arrival, dinner conversation doesn't center on Gracie. My parents skillfully turn the talk to Chuck and me. In their attentiveness, the gentle encouragement behind each question, I feel the years roll back to my own childhood. The sense of relief grows. In taking on the mantle of parental care, they *are* returning to themselves. And I wonder how much of my relief stems from love, how much from selfish happiness. I'm middle-aged, a mother myself, but I still want to be their child.

Chuck fills them in on the screenplay he wrote based on his first book. He's giving them the funny version, the stories about being asked to put in more sex, the out-of-the-blue cell-phone calls from the actor who will star.

When my turn comes, I talk about the 9/11 book. For the first time since I started writing fiction, I tell them, I've ignored the impulse to change things.

"It seems important to stick close to the reality I remember," I say.

"So it's a memoir?" my mother asks.

"Kind of."

As if my admission caused a shift in conversational gears, we begin to talk about 9/11. Wait, I want to say, writing isn't reality, no matter how close the writer may try to stick to it. I'm creating strings of words to wrap ideas in. Claiming to do anything else would be a lie.

Instead of protesting, though, I offer Gracie an asparagus spear, which she pushes away, and listen to Chuck describe what he saw from the roof. With a start, I realize he's never told me before. History came crashing down before we could compare notes.

"Someone had a pair of binoculars," he's saying. "Through

them you could see the jumpers. When he offered me a look, I couldn't take him up on it. I just couldn't witness those deaths."

He stares at his hands, which are splayed on the tablecloth. All of us, even Gracie, look at them, too.

"Everyone deals with it differently," he says.

FIRE (JUNE 12)

The air is so dry that when one of us moves across the sheets at night, the darkness crackles with sparks.

The cholla cactus in the backyard unfolds sticky magenta flowers, but my parents' front lawn is burnt to straw. Santa Fe is under a strict water-rationing regimen. Drought possibly caused by global warming has led to a rash of forest fires throughout the West. Ninety thousand acres near Cimarron are in flames. The same number burn out of control around Denver.

In the afternoon, Chuck and I take the Taos Highway north to visit Arthur and Carol and their daughter, who's Gracie's age.

A crescent moon skims the horizon. The pale valley shines below. I love this drive, I tell my husband. You can see almost to the Colorado border.

At the top of Tesuque Hill we spot smoke rising above the mountains. A thick white rope twisting into an anvil cloud, the smoke looks like a thunderhead tied to the earth by a string.

"You see that?" I murmur.

The question is unnecessary, since Chuck, too, is staring at the plume.

Tears flood my eyes.

"What is it?" His voice is low with tension.

"The Colorado fire?"

"Can't be," he says. "It's too close."

Though the plume is larger and lighter in color, it's the vision of the cloud that filled the downtown sky on September 11.

At first the sensations aren't linked to language. My chest hurts. It's hard to breathe. Then the words come. *Death is here. We're going to die.*

This, I realize, must be an anxiety attack. All I know is I have to keep it together because I'm at the wheel, with my family in the car. *Breathe*, I tell myself. Without thinking, I breathe the way I was taught in order to endure labor, one long inhalation, two short puffs out. Slowing, I opt not to pull over. Tesuque Hill's a killer, and we're on the downhill curve, where the highway is flanked by deep arroyos. Cars and trucks speed past. It's safer to stay on the road.

"I think I'm having a flashback," I tell Chuck.

"I think I am, too."

We're quiet. I concentrate on staying within the solid and broken lines.

Finally we reach the bottom. At Tesuque Pueblo, the foothill wilderness parts to reveal the Cities of Gold Casino. The casino's vast parking lot is bright with the beetle backs of pickup cabs and cars.

Soon we descend so low we no longer can see the smoke. Like the setting moon, it has disappeared.

SECURITY (JUNE 13)

Dense black clouds hang over the Sangre de Cristos. Their smoky undersides flicker and pulse red, reflecting the fire that burns below. It's as if we're seeing a thunderstorm lit by otherworldly lightning. Gods at war.

"Hell might look like that," Chuck says.

We're standing on the deck of the mountainside spa where we've spent a luxurious afternoon. Both of us wear kimonos with our locker keys pinned to the belts. I've been trying to shut off my mind and just relax, but it's hard not to feel the moment's absurd irony. While we sip from glasses of purified water with cucumber and lemon slices floating in them, the hills around us are burning.

A white woman with skin made leathery by years of sun steps out onto the deck with us. Instead of a kimono, she has on khaki shorts and a green T-shirt. Running a hand through her cropped hair she says, "The fire's at Cow Creek. Five hundred acres as of this morning."

How does she know?

She lives there, at Cow Creek.

"I'm not worried about the house. The fire's spreading to the north, and we're south of it. Besides," she says, grinning, "we live near a bunch of rich people. They won't let rich people's houses burn."

Though we're costumed in the spa's robes, it must be clear we're not to be numbered among the rich. When the woman turns to go, the word "Security," printed in a darker green against the green of her shirt, flashes from her back.

And now it's night. A breeze makes my parents' wind chimes ring like temple bells. Pine smoke fills the air. Santa Fe is circled by fire. We are surrounded by flames, but under the *portal* my father is doing the crossword puzzle while my mother and husband read.

Inside with my sleeping daughter, I open my notebook. I'm tempted to call the moment a metaphor for the times. I could take heart in the persistence of daily life or bemoan human blindness.

Instead, I listen to the wind chimes and watch my daughter's chest rise and fall.

Repetition (June 16)

Another fire has blazed to life in the wilderness near the city.

It's the morning of our last full day in New Mexico. Except for the smoke dusting the horizon, the sky is a clear pale blue. We're at Salvador Perez Playground, where we've arranged to meet Carol, Arthur, and their daughter. The girls are sitting in the castle's crosshatched shade eating crackers, which Gracie doles out to her friend one at a time.

When the firefighting helicopter flies by, it passes so low we can see the bucket trailing behind it. The rope bowing against the wind seems as thin as a thread, the bucket no larger than a garden pail.

Gracie and Lian stare at the sky, and I wonder how so little slurry can possibly make a dent in a forest fire. Fire in dry pine is a holocaust. Everything is consumed.

"It's a helicopter," I tell them.

"Like Herky," Gracie says.

"Who?" asks Carol.

"Herky the Helicopter. From *Jay-Jay the Jet Plane.*"

"It looks like a dragonfly about to mate," Chuck says.

"How?" I ask, remembering again why I love him.

"You know," he says. "When they bend their tails to touch."

A few minutes later a second helicopter passes over us, its shadow rippling over the green-gray leaves of the cotton-woods near the parking lot. By now it's clear that the playground lies directly below the flight path between the fire and refueling ground. A propeller plane goes by, followed by a third helicopter with suspended pail.

With each flyover, Gracie grows more excited.

"Oh, look at it!" Rising from the sand, she whirls one hand round and round in imitation of the revolving blades.

It is repetition, a gradual accrual of the known, that has whipped her into this happy state.

And I wish I could share her joy, but for me repetition has the opposite effect. These days, it makes disaster seem inevitable.

FATHER'S DAY (JUNE 16)

My father is shaving. From where I stand in the hall, the bathroom, lit by sun pouring down from the skylight, seems neon bright.

He's wearing his boxers but no undershirt. The Band-Aid at the base of his spine is fully exposed. It covers the incision from a biopsy of a suspicious mole taken two days ago. Yesterday he was supposed to wash the site with peroxide, then leave it exposed to air.

Without knocking I walk into the bedroom, where my mother is brushing her hair.

"Mom," I say, "Dad's still got the Band-Aid on."

She smiles tiredly up at me. "Could you do it, Jocey?"

When I understand she's asking me to tend to my father's wound, I hesitate. Sheepishly, I realize I want her to take responsibility. I want her to fix it, to make everything better.

"Sure," I say.

"Honey?" she shouts at my father.

"Dad?" I call. "I'll be right there."

Rummaging through the linen closet, I find the cotton balls and brown bottle of hydrogen peroxide.

My father turns toward me. One cheek is still covered with shaving cream.

"It's time to dress the incision, Dad."

"Thanks," he says, then turns back to the mirror.

Though he's almost seventy, my father has the lean torso of a much younger man. I can't remember the last time I touched his bare back. The moment is buried deep in childhood.

Cautiously, I tug at the Band-Aid. The peach-colored adhesive cloth is pale against his dark skin. It's made of a heavier gauge than the usual drugstore brands. Stickier. I have to pull.

"Sorry."

He flinches but doesn't answer. What's bothering me, I realize, is his acquiescence. He doesn't protest that he can clean the wound himself, he simply presents his body, like the patient he's become.

The lesion is the size of a dime. About a half an inch of flesh has been scooped out. The small crater is red around the edges, the white tissue underneath veined with the roots of the mole that proves to be benign, though we won't know till days later. I hadn't realized how far down the dark roots go. Like fissures in marble, they seem to be a part of him.

Gracie walks in, stares at her grandfather's back.

"Grandpa has a boo-boo," I calmly tell her. "I'm going to put some medicine on it."

When I pass the soaked cotton ball over the crater, a streak of peroxide drips down to the top of his shorts.

"Black medicine," Gracie says. "Mommy's putting black medicine on Grandpa's boo-boo."

A few minutes later, I corner my mother alone in the kitchen.

"Are you sure you don't remember the first time you saw the mole change?" I ask.

It seems crucial to recover the early warning signs. She doesn't remember, though, and doesn't seem perturbed by the lapse.

"Don't worry, honey," she says. And I'm left to wonder about my own sense of urgency. Would knowing when the change came play a role in possible treatment? Probably not. My need to know has to do with fear. If you can trace the path back from catastrophe, you might be able to avoid it next time—or magically undo the damage done.

My mother gazes meaningfully at me. Her eyes, I realize for the first time, are the exact same shade of hazel as Gracie's.

"Don't worry, honey," she says again. "There's no use worrying until there's something to worry about."

She gets herself another cup of coffee. She drinks it black now, instead of with the splash of skim milk she's poured for years. My mother has changed, too. She has learned the lesson of emotional economy—a lesson that, I imagine, allows her to go on.

OLD MEN AND MONSTERS (JUNE 17)

While Chuck tries to convince the Kansas City airport screener that the round-edged toddler knife in our bag poses no threat, I run past the gates after Gracie.

By New Mexico time it's two-thirty in the afternoon, an hour past her nap time. She's tired and in no mood to listen to my pleas and commands. Finally reaching her, I swing her into my arms. Boarding for our connecting flight has already begun. I've been up since 4 A.M. If I were less tired and tense I'd laugh, turning her capture into a game. Instead my face is stony, my eyes cold. Gracie starts to wail. Twisting away from me, she slides to the dirty gray industrial carpet, where she weeps and writhes.

A large family—the oldest girl wheels her own Barbie carry-on—divides, then walks around my howling child. Desperately I glance at Chuck. He's still talking to the screener, an elderly man with pink skin.

The last call for boarding is being loudly announced. The budget airline we're flying has open seating, so we may have lost the chance to sit together. Watching the pink guard's mouth move, it dawns on me that we might even miss our plane.

Finally Chuck is allowed to gather our possessions and move on. The moment he comes over, Gracie stops crying.

While we stand in line, Chuck tells me that the toddler knife survived but the scissors he used for trimming his beard and the small penknife on my key chain were confiscated.

I'm sorry about the penknife, which my parents gave me for Christmas years ago. The handle, made by a Zuñi jeweler, was inlaid with turquoise and mother-of-pearl. I had carried it with me for so long I'd forgotten it might be seen as a weapon.

"We're traveling stupidly," I say.

We are. How could I have been so careless as to let us fly with scissors and knives? Even a knife so blunt it barely cuts butter can't be excused, not when box cutters turned planes into guided bombs.

On board we miraculously find three empty seats across. I set Gracie down near the window, then help Chuck stow our gear—the laptops, diaper bag, backpacks, and food—under the seats in front of us.

Gradually I become aware that someone is talking to me.

"That's my seat," he says.

A pink-skinned old man—can he be the screener's brother?—is glaring down at me. He's very tall, with bloodshot blue eyes.

"Your seat?"

"My seat. I put my magazine there to save it."

Following the path of the accusatory finger, I see that Gracie is holding a magazine open on her lap, only it isn't a magazine but a pamphlet, the long narrow kind used for religious tracts or product warranties. She's "reading" it aloud, happily announcing whatever words come to mind.

"That's my magazine," the man is saying.

"You know," Chuck gently says, "moving one little magazine is a whole lot easier than moving all this stuff and a small child."

"It's my seat. I saved it."

Chuck meets my eyes, then bends to collect our belongings. Soon he's working his way down the crowded aisle.

Trying to hide my frustration, I reach for Gracie. Because the man is still glaring at me, I say, "It was a mistake."

I'd meant the words as equal parts disclaimer and apology, but they come out edged with anger.

"It wasn't a mistake. You did it on purpose."

Gracie begins to sob.

"You fucking asshole," I hear myself say. "You senile old fool."

He reaches over the back of the seat. When I realize that he's trying to wrestle the pamphlet away from Gracie, I rip it from her grasp, then fling it in his face.

One of my hands is clamped around his forearm. The skin sliding loosely over the bone feels soft and cool.

"Don't you dare touch her!" I hiss.

"I didn't."

He has gone from bristling to blank. His blotchy face appears to be made out of clay. It's now clear that he's exactly what I accused him of being, a senile old man.

Stalking deeper into the cabin with my frightened, weeping daughter clinging to my neck, I wonder how I became such a monster.

AFTER THE RAIN (JUNE 22)

Pools of water gleam on the thruway's shoulders. Mist rises from the trees. It's been five days since we flew back east, but I'm still getting used to dark green mountains wet with rain.

Our tires sluice over the pavement. We're driving back from Chuck's Uncle Vinny's eightieth birthday party, near Pough-keepsie. Vinny is recovering from triple-bypass surgery. Everyone in the extended family silently bowed to the need to gather for one last big bash.

Vinny's semidetached condo was so crammed with people and steaming food that even central air conditioning couldn't cool it down. The place was steeped in the bric-a-brac sadness of old Queens, where Chuck and I grew up and where Vinny and his wife, Connie, lived before retiring.

Driving out of the subdivision, we passed row upon iden-tical row of aluminum-sided houses. Young grass furred the raw earth of the newer yards. The few sticklike saplings home-owners had thought to plant wouldn't cast shade for years.

"This is where working-class white people from the city move to feel safe," Chuck said.

Raindrops peppered the windshield.

"Nowhere is safe." I'd spoken without thinking. The sen-tence seem to come not from me but from somewhere beyond me. In this way, the idea took on the weight of a rev-elation.

Nowhere is safe. I no longer believe in refuge. During the past year, I stopped thinking we could hide. It's impossible to stand apart from the world. I can't do it; the nation can't do it. Borders and oceans mean nothing. We were attacked and can be again, but the end of refuge means more than that. The pain we inflict on others has become our own.

And now the storm is over. The mist-covered Catskills are a gray screen on which I see the burning forests of the West, the World Trade towers' smoking ruins, bombed ruins that could be anywhere.

Gracie is asleep, so I let myself drowse. When I snap back awake, we've almost reached our exit.

"Slow around this turn," I murmur.

JULY 3

Because today is the day before the Fourth of July, firecrackers and Roman candles pop and whine in the otherwise quiet night.

I'm in my studio, the shed behind the pump house that used to be a shop. The long wooden table where I sit bears vise-clamp scars at both ends. Stacks of two-by-fours and coffee cans filled with nails and screws are arranged on the shelves behind it.

Being in the presence of tools that make useful things often inspires me, but tonight the charm doesn't work. I'm not sure how to reenter my book. It's too peaceful here. Away from the city that's my subject, I don't know what to write about.

I long to be in that other world, caught up in the act of writing.

Suddenly there's a deep boom, an explosion so loud it rumbles in my chest.

Again, my body tells me. *It's happening again.*

A couple of seconds later there's another boom, and another. Pushing the screen door open, I step out into the darkness. Three bright rectangles are all I see of the cabin. Another boom resounds. The sky in the east flashes white. When the light fades, it leaves an afterimage of cutout trees.

When the first plane struck the World Trade Center, we thought the sound signaled a construction accident at a site a few blocks north of us. "That was so loud someone might have died," Chuck said. He wanted to turn on the news right away, but I said we shouldn't bother. They wouldn't have the story yet, I told him.

My flashlight beam weakly skims the grass. Inside the house, Chuck's lying on the couch reading.

"Fireworks," I say. "My guess is the neighbors near the road."

"They're the likely suspects."

He lays down his book. The gold leaf on the spine has worn thin, but I can still make out the title.

"Whitman's Civil War journals?"

"You should read it when I'm through."

Chuck wears the quiet expression of someone deep inside a good book. Immersed in Walt Whitman's prose, he wasn't shaken by the explosions. Enviously, I think of my own book waiting unfinished in the shed. Writing carried me through the worst of mourning. Finding the right words kept me from being too badly seared. It let me see without going blind.

Walking past my husband, I lean into the bedroom to check on Gracie. The moment my shadow falls across her, she starts to yell.

"No!" she shouts. "No, not!"

When I reach down to ease her from the nightmare, I discover she's still sound asleep.

II
WHAT ISN'T THERE

Now I say that the peace the spirit needs is peace,
not lack of war, but fierce continual flame.
—MURIEL RUKEYSER

WHAT ISN'T THERE

(MARCH AND FEBRUARY 2003)

WHAT IS LOST

1

Every time I cross Second Avenue, I glance downtown at a sky that's empty of the two towers.

For most of my life—all of my life in Manhattan—the World Trade towers were my south. They were as much a part of the landscape as mountains would be if New York City had mountains. They were as actual as mountains; more than actual, rising from the imaginary map I saw in my head whenever I thought of home.

What is lost, then, is the feeling of being at home. The ground I live on isn't solid, isn't fully real. If mountains can vanish, nothing can be taken as given.

2

Green flames streak the night sky above Baghdad. A building disappears into dust. It was, we are told, part of a governmental complex.

The void where the building stood is now filled with green paper. Hundreds of thousands of sheets of paper float down in a spiraling waterfall. Caught by a burning updraft, they swirl high, only to flutter down again.

Shock and Awe, it's being called.

On September 11, hundreds of thousands of sheets of paper were broadcast through the air, too. Each one contained words that were, in a single moment of violence, ripped out of their contexts. Never to be read again, they stopped being words. They drifted over us, alighting on the East River like petals, like the flowers mourners toss after consigning the ashes to water.

3

What isn't there, in all the hours I've watched TV since the war started six days ago, is any real accounting of the Iraqi dead.

"It would be presumptuous of me to say," says a cheerful-looking major general dressed in khaki fatigues.

He has just been asked to provide a number. The journalist who did the asking is one of many gathered in a large room that may, in fact, be a tent. All wear outfits like T-shirts and khaki shorts, the casual clothing of desert war.

The major general turns the journalists' attention and thus ours to the TV screen next to him. The tent room vanishes. The scene before us now is a gray moonscape of pockmarked sand. Black crosshairs hover over a dark blob.

"Here we have an armored personnel carrier," the major general says.

The blob grows larger, then silently turns into a puff of gray dust. When the gray cloud clears, the blob is gone.

During the first Gulf War, the Iraqis who were killed were known as "collateral damage." Now they aren't known as anything at all. They have been completely unnamed.

Armored personnel carrier. There is no language to enshroud them.

4

What isn't there, not anymore, is my will to write, my will to do much of anything.

Home from school, I walk into the living room where my husband, still in his bathrobe, is watching the news. It's a few minutes past two in the afternoon. Without a word, I drop the *Times* onto the couch between us, then sit down.

They're talking about casualties now. One hundred fifty Iraqi soldiers lie dead on the banks of the Euphrates. Twelve civilians are killed as bombs tear apart a Baghdad marketplace. The screen fills with an indecipherable tangle of tan and blue-gray cloth: the bodies of four U.S. servicemen. Beneath them runs a line of words that flows away as fast as rain sliding over glass.

The war that's not a war is called "Operation Iraqi Freedom." Deconstructing the name does nothing to negate its awful absurdity. At the peace marches and rallies we attended before the invasion began, I was cheered up by the clever signs—"Regime Change Starts at Home," "Bombing

Iraq Is *So* 1990's"—but in this moment find myself unable to concoct a single slogan in self-defense.

My heart is broken. I'm ashamed to be an American. I can't even face the forum of my notebook.

5

It's not just the war. The slow erosion of my voice—the quiet voice I use when I talk to myself on the page—began the summer before, while the country braced for the first anniversary of 9/11.

I found I had nothing to say about that solemn Fourth of July, nothing to say about the memorial events or plans to build on the World Trade Center site. Any attempt to circle toward meaning still felt dangerously flawed. So many lives had been pounded to dust. Workers in white moon suits raked through the dust for bone fragments, a splintered tibia, a fingertip, shards of scapulas and skulls. The world around us was shattered. I was shattered. Trying to gather fragments seemed the only reasonable response.

On the morning of September 11, 2002, I took Gracie to the Lower East Side for her first day of nursery school. The large room was loud with primary colors. Gracie poured fine white sand onto a blue Ferris wheel, then watched it spin. The other two-year-olds around her played with blocks, puzzles, and toy telephones while their parents or baby-sitters sat in tiny chairs, their knees bent like long-legged spiders.

The tall west windows, I realized, must have framed the World Trade Towers.

Answering my question, Maria, the lead teacher, said, "We saw everything. Luckily the parents were still here, so they could take the children home."

Suddenly the idea of leaving my daughter in this happy room a full mile away from our apartment seemed unbearable.

At 8:46 A.M., the minute the first plane struck the first tower, I reached for Liselot's hand, then closed my eyes. Perky music drifted around us, a song about little ducks. When I opened them again, the fluorescent lights were too bright, surrounding the objects they lit with pulsing auras. Several other mothers also had joined hands, and bent their heads as if in prayer.

Everything was wrong. Though the gesture was spontaneous and deeply felt—I'd grasped Liselot's hand and closed my eyes just to survive the moment—it now seemed trite, false. The melodrama of our clasped hands and bowed heads embarrassed me. Later I'd realize why. It was as if someone had claimed the tableau and made it stand for an America united by grief, united in Christ, prepared to wage war, sternly braced for Armageddon. Even our pain wasn't ours.

In the months after September 11, I've read countless essays, articles, editorials, speeches, poems, and stories trying to make sense of the day. But words have gotten away from me. In a time when slaughter is called "liberation," nouns that once stood for things have become lies. Lies from the government are nothing new, but these latest lies seem to have undone our language by denying the possibility of variant readings. Layered meanings, the sweet subversions borne by each word, don't seem possible anymore. I don't how to tell my truths. With all the talk of evil and good, to say "What if?" becomes a crime.

Through it all, I somehow still believed I could shield the soft voice I hear when I talk to myself on the page—the voice that tells me things I never thought of, in words that are and aren't mine—but then the screen darkened with the first bombs of war.

6

When I was a young woman, just out of college, living alone in New Mexico, my house was burglarized.

The house stood at the edge of a hayfield. Each growing-season night, I fell asleep to the hush-rush of the acequia flowing past my bedroom window. One afternoon I found a pale green scorpion on the bed and, unsure whether it was the poisonous kind, trapped it in a jar. When the scorpion sensed what I'd done, it skittered frantically around, trying to find a way out. Green claw tapping curved glass, it measured the limits of its newly circumscribed world.

On the day I was burglarized, I came home from the office of the newspaper where I worked to find that my electric typewriter and radio were gone. Also missing was my sleeping bag, which I kept unzipped on the bed for a quilt.

Nothing else I owned was worth stealing, unless you counted the books.

It turned out that my sole set of bed sheets was missing, too. He—the burglar had to have been a man—probably used them to carry off the stolen goods, said the police officer who came to investigate my case.

The theft of the sheets, the things of least value, disturbed me the most. Wrapped in them, I'd given myself over to sleep, left myself open and vulnerable. For many nights afterward, I had insomnia. It was no longer safe to sleep, to dream. The country of my dreaming had been invaded.

In the year and a half since September 11, I've come to understand that physical destruction was just the beginning. The mountains are gone, and in their place hangs a haze of death. Instead of dispersing, the haze has grown denser, spreading over America's heart. It has drifted across oceans to Afghanistan, the Middle East, Southeast Asia, Iraq. It promises to drift till it covers the world.

The taking of lives will not end. The taking of words. Stolen dreams.

Experiencing Silence (March 7)

The door at the end of the corridor seems strangely naked.

The door is the door to my office at school. It's naked because someone, I realize, has torn down the two antiwar posters that my colleague Jim and I taped there last week. On one poster, the word "war" was slashed through in red, like a no-smoking sign, by the word "Inspections." On the other was the slogan "War is a weapon of mass deception."

This, I automatically think, is an outrage, a violation of our right to free speech. I'll have to complain to our department chair, then e-mail the university's president. The idea tires me. Dealing with the signs' disappearance is one more chore in a crowded teaching day.

Before anything, though, I have to make the calls. My assigned time to begin phoning senators is 9:23 A.M.

When I dial, however, the line is busy. I hit redial, and again the busy signal beeps. While waiting to get through, I log on to the Web site of the peace organization leading the virtual protest, a "march" on Washington consisting of a flood of phone calls and e-mail messages protesting the imminent war on Iraq. Materializing on my computer screen is a map of the United States. The familiar shape of the nation is sliced into states identified by two or three letters apiece. Pop-up boxes proclaiming why the U.S. should not invade Iraq cover the East Coast side.

The map, I soon see, lacks any real reference to geography. The space within its black borders is free of rivers or mountains. There are no cities. The United States of America hovers alone, unchained from Canada and Mexico. Even the oceans are gone.

The effect is unintentional, but the stripped-down map seems to stand for the isolationism that helped give rise to this whole mess in the first place.

After the tenth or eleventh try, I finally get through. A young man—his voice glistens with youth—says hello, tells me I've reached Senator Clinton's office. I say hello back, and give my name and the name of the city where I live. Then I recite the brief statement I wrote last night, the same statement I posted earlier to the peace group's Web page and that undoubtedly floats in one of the pop-up boxes over New York.

As I pronounce the words, I can almost see them, in bold-face Times New Roman. I wonder if the young intern is typing my statement or in any way recording it. Maybe he's making another check mark in the "no" column under "war." Maybe he's doing nothing, not even listening.

"Thank you for calling," he says. "I'll give the senator your message."

Dialing the next number on the list, I go through the same routine.

Soon it's time to call the president. Surprisingly, I get through right away. A recorded voice, a man's, thanks me for calling the White House message line, then informs me that I'll be put on hold.

"George Bush wants to know what you think," the voice says, then adds, "While you wait, you will experience silence."

Experience silence? As promised, no sound issues from the receiver. I can't help feeling a little surprised. Most businesses pipe in canned music to those on hold. Why this nothingness, which seems chintzy, given the source? Perhaps the powers that be debated about music but couldn't decide which style best represented America. Classical was too elitist, easy listening too lame, jazz too beat, rap too black. Country? Muzak? John Philip Sousa? Silence was more dignified. It wouldn't offend, and besides there was the added advantage of keeping the caller on edge. With silence on the end of the line, it would be impossible to tell if you were still connected, or if the connection had been severed long ago.

Boxes of words have begun to pop up over the West Coast and country's interior. America is waking up.

When the phone silence finally ends, I'm told I am permitted to speak. Once again I declare my name and city. Clearly and slowly, as if leaving a message on a dentist's voice mail, I say that so-called preemptive war is in and of itself an act of terror and that I don't want my tax dollars used to fund terrorism.

The statement, which seemed mildly clever the night before, has been stripped of all meaning. Somehow, the silence knocked the living voice out of me.

It's not just that my words will remain unheard. I don't really expect the message to be played back. Besides, I've got practice here. I've written thousands of pages no one will ever see: early drafts, stories, essays, and God knows what else that was born dead in the water.

But even the flattest sentences carried in them the seeds of a life beyond mine.

Deflated, I set down the phone. Glancing at my watch, I see that nine minutes remain till my first student conference,

enough time to run to the cafeteria for a cup of coffee before
the onslaught begins.

FILLING THE GAP (MARCH 5)

The march will begin with a candlelight vigil, and I've come
prepared. In a plastic bag tucked in the stroller are the Shabbat
candles we used for last Halloween's jack-o'-lantern and the
paper Tweety Bird cups left over from Gracie's third birthday
party.

It's a Wednesday, at rush hour, dusk. The demonstrators are
crowded onto the Midtown sidewalks, fenced in by police
sawhorses and silver rails. While we wait for the darkness to
deepen, I poke holes through the bottoms of the cups, then
push in the stubby candles. Chuck helps me light them.

The result isn't exactly what I'd envisioned. The candles
are too short, the cartoon cups too opaque to let much light
through. My candles for peace look like lopsided Disney ice
pops. I hand them around anyway, to Chuck, our friend
Hettie, and a couple of women standing nearby. Finally, I give
an unlit candle-and-cup combo to Gracie.

"No!" she howls. "I want real fire!"

"Real fire might burn you, honey."

This is her first peace rally. Ever since Chuck and I started
marching last month, Gracie has begged to come along. Like
fire, protests are part of the mysterious grown-up world. Some
mysteries should remain mysterious, but this time we decided

to take her. We wanted her to begin to understand the need for peace. Which meant, I realized, defining war.

"War is when many people hurt many other people," I told her. "Do you think that's a good idea?"

Eyes wide with semi-staged awe, she answered, "It's bad to push and hit. You must say, 'No, stop, I don't like that.'"

Chuck and I liked saying that our three-year-old knew more about human decency than George W. Bush.

Now she hurls her cup and candle to the ground.

"I know you're angry," I say, "but you can't have fire. Would you like something to eat instead?"

Though I'd promised myself never to become the kind of mother who pacifies a child with food, I open a plastic container and take out a hard-boiled egg. Gracie's pudgy fingers leave gray streaks on the glossy globe. After she takes a few bites, the egg shoots out onto the sidewalk. Before I can retrieve it, along with the abandoned Tweety Bird candle, a man in an orange ski jacket takes a step backward, smashing it flat.

Gracie begins to sob.

"Poor girl," says a woman with short black hair.

Smiling, Hettie leans down, then rattles the tambourine she's brought along. I find a second egg and some carrot sticks.

"Where's my other glove?" Hettie says, half to herself.

Chuck finds it in the gutter, all but submerged in a black puddle. The leather fingertips curl in the imploring gesture of someone caught in the act of drowning.

★　★　★

After Gracie finishes eating, I hand her her own toy tambourine.

"Let's make some music, baby!" Hettie sings.

On the other side of the sawhorses, a policewoman cheerfully calls to my daughter, "Hey, tambourine girl. Are you my tambourine girl?"

The hair stuffed under her regulation cap is braided into cornrows. She's plump, busty, maybe a mother herself. If she were anything but an officer charged with controlling the crowd, I'd smile back and chat with her.

The protesters start to shuffle forward.

This is the moment we've been waiting for. Shuffling along, I feel like cheering. There's power in the crowd's slowness, a slowness born of our numbers. Maybe the path toward war, the black-and-white silent-film conveyor belt inching us toward the fire, isn't the one the nation's doomed to take. We're not helpless. We have a voice.

A chant ripples through the crowd. "What do we want? Peace! When do we want it? Now!" A woman yelps when the newspaper cone around her candle dissolves in flames. The chant grows louder. Most of us are respondents, shouting the antiphonal words "peace" and "now." Something's off, though. The familiar chant doesn't quite scan. While the U.S. military is poised to invade, hostilities against Iraq haven't yet officially begun. If peace can be defined as an absence of war, technically we have it, at least in Iraq.

And now a man in a tailored black suit comes dancing

across the avenue. He's wearing a George Bush mask and blood-covered rubber hands with long black nails. His were-wolf paws clasp a green-and-white beach-ball globe. Pointing at it with one reddened claw, he growls, "Mine!"

"He's scary," Gracie says.

"Yes, he is, sweetie."

We're walking quickly now. Marchers have fanned out down Broadway. At the next intersection, a cop in a reflective vest waves us to a stop. Obediently, we wait while a long line of cars goes by. The protesters ahead of us have kept on walking. Uneasily I watch them drift away. Without the united force of the crowd, we're just a bunch of people holding candles and signs.

At the next crosswalk waits a group of women and men who must be the march's organizers. One man has scaled a traffic-light pole. Holding on to the "Don't Walk" sign, he leans out over the street.

"Don't let them break you up!" he shouts. "There's a gap! Try to fill it!"

Chuck takes over pushing the stroller. Hettie and Gracie beat their tambourines faster. But before long, we have to stop to take Gracie to a coffee-shop bathroom. A few minutes later we stop again to buy her a juice box. By the time we reach Fourteenth Street, we've drifted to the ragged end of the line.

Glancing back, I notice that we're not at the actual end. A phalanx of police officers brings up the rear. Moving with the grace that authority brings, they march in a dark, uniform line.

They've been here all along. As if they were the force impelling us.

One of them catches my eye, the same policewoman who called to our daughter at the beginning. When she sees that I see her, she slowly waves a black-gloved hand.

"Hey, tambourine girl," she says. "How's my tambourine girl doing?"

In the Distance (February 15)

Gracie strides into the kitchen. Looking up at the familiar faces, the relatives and friends who crowd around the table, she says, "What is in the distance?"

Only about half of the grown-ups hear her. Some are sipping coffee or eating bagels. Most watch Hettie, who's showing off the capes, sweaters, and hats, the many layers she plans to wear against the cold.

"Excuse me, this is not a joke," Gracie says. "What is in the distance?"

Her Uncle Ed and Aunt Lori glance out the window, into the distance just named. The others turn to look, too. I stare at Midtown's skyscrapers. Within an hour, all of the adults in the room will be standing before the United Nations with thousands of other protesters. I'm not a little afraid. However hard I've tried to resist them, the government's terror alerts have worked their spell. Stowed in our cabinets are duct tape, plastic, masks, talismans against attack. Dirty and conventional bombs aren't my only concern. My post-9/11 fear of heights and planes lately has been joined by a new fear, of open spaces. Agoraphobia. I'm afraid of the agora, the public square—the very place, figuratively speaking, where we'll soon gather to express our collective will.

"Where in the distance? What do you see, baby?" Hettie asks.

"No, nothing." Gracie's lower lip juts out in a pout.

She has asked the same question over and over the past couple of days, so I know she's not referring to any specific thing in the distance, but to the concept of distance itself. Her father and I have tried to explain. None of our answers satisfy her.

"Distance is when something is very far away," Chuck says now.

"How do you go in the distance?"

"There are many ways. You can drive a car or take a train or bus or plane. Or you can walk, if you walk for a long, long time."

Gracie shakes her head. "Where is in the distance?" she tries again.

Reaching down, I pull her onto my lap. Gazing into her eyes, I say, "In the distance is anywhere far away from you. When you get there, it's no longer distant. Distance moves. It's always changing, beautiful girl."

She slides out of my embrace. I have given her another explanation that explains nothing. It's true that the more I grapple with the question, the less sure I am of the answer. What *is* in the distance? Can anyone really say?

We arrive an hour early, but the closest we can come is the corner of Fifty-fifth Street and First Avenue, six long uptown blocks from the stage near the United Nations building.

It's freezing. The crowd presses around us, and I'm glad we left Gracie with her sitter at home. Metal gates line the curb. In a reversal of the usual pedestrian rules, we're supposed to stay on the street, keeping the sidewalks clear. The wide avenue keeps filling with people. Soon the crowd stretches all the way to the Fifty-ninth Street Bridge. Counting the blocks on gloved fingers, I calculate that we're right in the middle of a solid mile of protesters. Later we'll learn that two hundred thousand gathered here, with tens or possibly hundreds of thousands more waiting outside the demonstration site.

I've never seen so many people in one place. Staring at the undulating waves of them on First Avenue, I can clearly trace the hills underneath the concrete, the hills that despite everything still shape our city. Like most New Yorkers, I don't think of Manhattan in geological terms. There is no north or south, no earth beneath us.

But now I see that we're part of the planet after all. Today, simultaneous rallies are being held in cities around the world, millions of us demanding peace. Standing in the cold with other New Yorkers around me, I discover that I'm no longer

afraid. Fear's absence feels like a sudden, literal lifting. As if a
hand pressing on my chest all these months has pulled away.

In the distance, the stage is a small black rectangle with a backdrop of colorful whorls. The speaker on it is a barely visible
dot. We can't hear a thing. A man standing nearby with a
boom box held balanced on his head has tuned the volume
loud, but to us the words are a jumble of sound. When my
sister-in-law Lori and I jiggle our radio dials, trying to find the
station that's simulcasting the rally, all we get is static.

The murmur begins from faraway, like a drumbeat, a pulse.
The chant has begun uptown, to the north. It grows louder,
rolling toward us, moving like an ocean swell. Before I can
hear the words, I hear the rhythm that embodies them, three
repeating beats, a choppy, tuneless waltz.

Finally the chant ripples closer. The people around us are
shouting in unison. "We want peace! We want peace! We want
peace!"

A low grinding noise is emanating from the flatbed truck
parked at the intersection. On the bed is a long white rectangle the size of a multiplex movie screen. The noise seems
to be coming from a mechanism that's slowly lifting and
turning the screen toward us. Suddenly, the screen flashes to
life. It is a screen after all, not just a metaphor I whipped up
in order to describe it. Till now I'd suspected it was a tool for
somehow controlling the crowd.

Bright colors move across the screen's surface. Soon they

resolve into the blue eyes and brown hair of a graffitied face. The image must be of the stage in front of the U.N., the very one we can barely see in real life.

The tremendous painted head dwarfs the head of the real man who stands before it. His bearded lips silently move. Like a practiced public speaker, the man looks to the left, then the right. His eyes gleam. He's passionate about what he's saying, only we still can't hear him. Watching his mouth, I think of TV screens soundlessly flashing in unlit rooms late at night, the lonely comfort of insomniacs.

Another chant is moving through the crowd. "We want sound! We want sound!"

The screen, which has been slowly rotating, grinds to a halt. It now fully faces us. Positioned against the building across the street, it looks like a huge window, as if a hole had been sliced through the cream-colored bricks to reveal the titans and their neon world on the other side.

A man's voice suddenly blares into existence, a voice so loud it can only belong to the televised giant.

He's calling on us to observe a moment of silence.

Bowing my head in an attitude of prayer, I think about how the screen's presence has changed everything. It has taken us closer to and farther away from the action. We can see and hear what's happening onstage, but we've stopped being as aware of the other people around us. If it weren't for the cold and pressed-together bodies, we all could be in our separate homes, watching the rally live on New York 1.

A muezzin's voice rings through the air.

"The call to prayer," Humera whispers.

I bow my head once again. The a cappella song sends a shiver through me. I've heard the same achingly beautiful melody issue from loudspeakers in the dollar stores on Fourteenth Street, and from our TV during broadcasts of the first Gulf War.

The voice is cool water flowing down my spine. Would the feeling of awe diminish or grow if I understood the words?

The bitter cold doesn't bother me at first, but gradually it radiates from the pavement into my soles, then my bones, till I'm stamping to stay warm.

"This is why pushcart vendors wear newspaper stuffed in their boots," Chuck is saying. "As insulation, it really works."

Like me, he's too cold to concentrate on what the onstage poets, politicians, activists, and actors are saying. He murmurs that we've been counted, that it's time to go. We have to get back to Gracie and Ping before the end-of-rally chaos sets in.

Working our way through the crowd, we reach an opening in the gates. When we finally break free, I look back. Long lines of metal rails, invisible while we stood between them, gleam in the sun like wet spider webs. The throng on the other side looks trapped. The feeling of having been in the midst of something powerful slightly fades.

"Keep moving," a cop tells us. "You can't stand here."

Walking west on Fifty-sixth Street, we pass brownstone

after brownstone. One upper-story window has been thrown open. A man in a thick white sweater stands at the open window. At first it seems as if he's trying to see the demonstration, but then I realize he's shouting.

"Traitors," he yells. "Traitors."

He repeats himself over and over. His voice, though loud, is strangely neutral. He's not really looking at us, not aiming the word our way.

The impersonality of his curse throws me. I don't know how to shout back.

At Second Avenue the police have erected another line of gates.

A cop lifts the rail aside so we can pass. Out of reflex, the good daughter, polite girl, I thank him.

"Don't," Chuck says.

On the other side, the street is alive with people. Unlike the vast crowd wedged into stillness one cross-town block away, the protesters here are in motion. They parade, wave signs, shout, chant, mill. Some bang bucket drums and sing.

"They won't let us in," a woman is saying. "They let people out but not in."

Glancing back, I see that four officers are guarding the gate we just walked through. The one I thanked is close enough to hear us, but he gives no sign of having done so. His face is impassive, eyes blank.

"It's a tactic to divide us, to keep the numbers down," the woman says. And I know she's not telling us because there's any remedy but because the story must be told. The evening's broadcasts and next day's papers won't mention it, I think. Instead they'll run versions of the rally and the other rallies around the world that erase the sensation of being there. The freezing cold. The joy. The undamageable power.

Weaving through knots of people, Chuck and I make our way downtown on Second Avenue. At Forty-ninth Street stand two long rows of cops in riot gear. They're at ease. Each holds a ropelike pair of white handcuffs.

Thinking of Gracie, I say, "We can't get arrested."

An officer riding a brown horse with blinders pushes into the crowd. And though I don't believe this day will stop the war from coming, I allow myself to hope. This must be what faith is: hope against unyielding reality, the telling of stories that must be told.

Epilogue

Like all journals, mine is given shape by the passage of time; like all journals, it is open-ended and must remain so. That the first part of the book stops short on July 3, 2002, is my deliberate attempt to circumvent closure. Besides, the war on Iraq was soon to deepen the wound, making closure impossible.

It seems appropriate, even necessary, to circle back to some of the words I chose to precede my own at the book's beginning. They are from the poet Mahmoud Darwish's account of the 1982 bombing of Beirut:

> I want to sing. I want a language that I can lean on
> and that can lean on me, that asks me to bear witness
> and that I can ask to bear witness, to what power
> there is in us to overcome this cosmic isolation.

During the summer of 2006, front-page photographs again presented the horror of the bombing of Beirut, among other cities in Lebanon. As I write this, the war in Iraq drags fatally on. In both countries the majority of victims were, and are, civilian. No journal of mine can even begin to touch on their suffering.

Medieval European chroniclers, guided by the Christian God lurking perpetually in the wings, recorded events they didn't necessarily have to understand or see the end of in order to describe. I can only imagine what it must have been like to write in the faith that sense would be made—to write knowing that after you finished, others would pick up where you left off. I pray for a future—though I can't foresee one—in which the story of 9/11, a tragedy that history keeps on writing, can find its place in the vast constellation of the world's stories and finally come to a close. It's in this spirit I ask readers to see *What Isn't There* as an early installment of an unfinished collaboration.

Acknowledgments

An earlier draft of "Shopping" appeared in *110 Stories: New York Writes after September 11*, edited by Ulrich Baer, published in 2002 by New York University Press.

The book's initial epigraphs are from a sermon by Gordon Dragt preached soon after 9/11 at Middle Collegiate Church in New York City, and from Mahmoud Darwish's *Memory of Forgetfulness: August, Beirut, 1982*, translated from the Arabic by Ibrahim Muhawi. The epigraph to the second section is from Muriel Rukeyser's poem "Easter Eve 1945," from *The Collected Poems*. Elsewhere in the book I quoted from the testimony of firefighter Joe Casaliggi, interviewed in *9/11*, the 2002 documentary directed by Jules Naudet, Gédéon Naudet, and James Hanlon.

I am grateful to Kathleen Anderson, Ruth Baldwin, Jeanne Boland, Jan Clausen, Gordon Dragt, Liz Gately, Jacqui Lewis, Carolyn Lieu, Noble Lieu, Michele Martin, Fiona McCrae, Susanne Michelis, Lorna Smedman, Johanna Veth-Abinusawa, and especially Chuck Wachtel for all that they did to help bring this book to life. I could not have written the memoir without my friends and family, and the neighbors and witnesses whose lives directly or indirectly touched my own.

For G.B. Fall,
in memory

www.ingramcontent.com/pod-product-compliance
Ingram Content Group UK Ltd.
Pitfield, Milton Keynes, MK11 3LW, UK
UKHW040305280225
455666UK00001B/6

9 781568 583464